3 STARTUPS, 40 PIVOTS

3 STARTUPS, 40 PIVOTS

HOW TO NOT F*CKING GIVE UP

ALI MOIZ   MURTAZA HUSSAIN

COPYRIGHT © 2026 ALI MOIZ, MURTAZA HUSSAIN

3 STARTUPS, 40 PIVOTS

*How to Not F*cking Give Up*

FIRST EDITION

ISBN   978-1-5445-5138-8   *Hardcover*
       978-1-5445-5137-1   *Paperback*
       978-1-5445-5139-5   *Ebook*

For Entrepreneurs and Founders everywhere.

ʃ ɔ •_• ʅʃ ɔ •_• ʅɔʃ ɔ •_• ʅɔʃ ɔ •_• ʅɔ

Take our energy

CONTENTS

FOREWORD

For a while, my thesis on angel investing was to find founders who would pivot, a lot.

My thinking was that you end up selecting for grit, intellectual honesty, low ego—some of the most important traits you want to see in any founder. So when Ali and Murti were starting their next company, I jumped on it, no questions asked. Seeing them pivot from a social network to an ad network and execute over six years to a successful exit in their last company as both a user (of Xuqa) and a customer (of Peanut Labs) convinced me that they had what it takes to do it again.

But even then, I wasn't prepared for quite how insane they were. It started off as HiGear: "Zipcar for Luxury Cars"—which I loved. Then they got their entire fleet robbed. Then I watched them pivot to a Slack competitor, an email marketing tool, and even a championship eSports team. At every turn I thought, *This has got to be it.*

But no—they kept going. And going. Like the Energizer Bunny. Almost 20 more pivots, over the course of a decade.

And eventually, they raised a huge round from the best investor in the world: Sequoia. And when the regulatory market shifted a few months later, they pivoted again. All the way to another successful exit to Logitech—as Streamlabs, which powered one third of all streamers in the world.

As Paul Graham observed when he started Y Combinator, startups are a test of intelligence. Hundreds of companies later, he realized that startups are a test of stamina. That's why when I think about my personal heroes as founders, I think about Ali and Murti. Getting a front-row seat to their journey has made me a better founder and has taught me what true resilience, patience, and flexibility looks like.

That story is what you are about to read in these pages.

—SIQI CHEN, FOUNDER, ANGEL INVESTOR

* * *

It's 2002 and I'm hunched in the back of Mr. Iqbal's chemistry class, the ceiling fan wheezing like an asthmatic camel, when Murti slides me a note: "We're calling it Gaming Ventura—cool?" Below the name he's already drawn a fake stock certificate. I later learn that Ali has a hot lead on our first prospect. We haven't learned valence electrons yet, but we've priced hosting at six bucks a month and decided Pepsi needs a gully-cricket league website. They laughed us out of the lobby.

Forty-eight hours later we're pitching their biggest rival—a tea company this time—a weight-loss portal, because nothing burns calories like rejection. That worked! First check: around 200 American dollars. We cashed it, bought knockoff x86 chips (because Intel was too expensive), and built an office in my dad's derelict storeroom downtown. I still remember we had two employees, one working elevator, and zero ventilation.

That summer we rented a trade-show booth to sell college

admissions courses. Catch: most of us hadn't even taken the SAT yet. Solution: recruit every good-looking friend we had, beg them to look pretty, and let hormones do the conversion. Sold every seat to eager dads, then lectured to a nearly empty ballroom at the Pearl Continental. Typical.

I think that was the same summer we tried to code an entire online office suite in Java at a cyber café where the PCs shut off every 45 minutes when the attendant microwaved his chai. Auto-save was prayer, and version control was yelling, "Did you email the file to yourself?" But we kept shipping, because that's what you do when the power flickers more than it stays.

So when I open this book and read about pivot 11, the hustle of trying to make things work, the 3:00 a.m. Stripe-decline emails, the acquisitions, I just laugh. Same two kids, different duct tape.

It's been inspirational to watch them build Peanut Labs, Streamlabs, Stonks—each exit bigger, each bet on themselves louder. They still conjure magic out of thin air, only now the invoices have commas and the payrolls create jobs across the world.

I know they won't linger on it here, but I've watched them funnel those winnings straight into the causes they never tweet about: classrooms for kids who still sit on the floor, rescue dogs who've never heard a kind word, founders who get their first check because two brothers remember what zero feels like. I know they don't do it for optics; I think they do it because generosity is the only revenge against chaos.

At the edge of 40 we can finally see the arc: two boys on a Karachi rooftop swapping knockoff processors for cricket tickets, now men on opposite ends of California still finishing each other's sentences. The brotherhood that started as "Don't tell Mom the monitor exploded" became "I'll get the Series B term sheet; you hire the engineers."

It's been an honor being their friend before the term sheets, before the commas, when the only thing we had to scale was hope. Here's to the next 40, boys. I'm fucking delighted to have been your friend through every version.

—ZAKI MAHOMED, FOUNDER

* * *

It was the height of summer, when most college students were chasing internships or killing time. We, on the other hand, were consumed by a different obsession: building a social network. Our first attempt, HotCampusParties.com, lit up Williams College with over 2,000 visitors in just days—almost the entire student body. But just as quickly, it fizzled. It wasn't truly viral.

One late night in Jesup Hall, we were determined to crack the code. Murti, always digging through the internet, stumbled upon Bebo—a once-huge social network that had been acquired for $500 million. He couldn't stop asking: how had Mike Birch pulled that off?

Hours passed as he and I combed through the site. No clear answers. Then came a bold move: Murti found Mike's number and called. To our surprise, Mike answered. He was warm, helpful, and shared a simple insight: "Build a bot that pulls contacts from Hotmail, Gmail, or wherever."

We jumped on it. In a few days, I built a bot that did exactly that. But when we launched, nothing happened. Others had already copied the same tactic. The trick had gone stale.

Then came the real insight: Facebook. It was exploding, already with millions of users. I scrapped the old bots and built one just for Facebook. Within hours, it was ready. Users would log in, the bot would pull their entire friend list, and ask: "Do you want to invite your friends to iVentster.com?" Over half said yes. Overnight, our user base shot from zero to 300,000.

A few days later, an investor reached out. Soon, $350,000 landed in our account. In just a week and a half, we'd built something that worked and secured funding—because we moved fast and didn't cling to what wasn't working.

But even that wasn't the end. iVentster eventually failed too. We pivoted again. And again. Over 10 times before we finally sold the company for $30 million.

That's the real lesson: pivots aren't just about ditching ideas. They're about running fast, focused experiments to find the right product, the right growth engine, and the right customer. Your idea isn't special until it works.

Ali and Murti became experts at this. The exits we had together prove it: relentless experimentation always, always wins.

The stories in these pages will help you build that same habit.

—PROSPER NWANKPA, THE 3RD MUSKETEER
& CTO/CO-FOUNDER, PEANUT LABS

* * *

Murti and Ali are two of the most relentlessly driven founders I've had the privilege to work with.

Our story began in June 2005, when we wired funds to iVentster—a college student events network started by Ali, Murti, and Prosper. They'd just graduated—or, in Murti's case, dropped out—of Williams College.

Within weeks, they were on a plane to Karachi, Pakistan, transferring our freshly raised funds halfway around the world. In the post-9/11 climate, I half-expected a knock from Homeland Security asking why a Silicon Valley VC had just financed an early-stage social network in Karachi.

A few weeks later, they shut it down entirely. "Too limiting," they told me. "We'll rebuild stronger."

I was livid. But that moment—equal parts audacity and clarity—set the pattern for everything that followed.

From the start, Ali and Murti were fast mutators: irreverent, allergic to convention, barefoot in boardrooms, able to pivot faster than most people process failure. They made iteration itself a core competency.

That first investment launched a two-decade relationship across four startups (we've backed three of them) defined by one principle: radical survivorship. When other founders would surrender, they'd reload. "Almost out of cash" became a rallying cry. When construction noise in their Karachi office threatened productivity, they called in family connections to bring in the police—only to have their neighbors call in the army to reinstate the noise.

Their second venture began as a peer-to-peer marketplace for exotic car rentals—firing on all cylinders until organized crime stole half the fleet in one night. An FTC shutdown followed later. Yet they kept iterating—through a dozen-plus pivots—until the next one landed and exited successfully.

Through all of it, one constant stood out: their devotion to their mother, who raised them as a single parent in Karachi. I suspect it was she who brokered peace between the police and the army that day 20 years ago.

Few founders test the boundaries of "impossible" the way they do. They'll break rules, burn orthodoxy, and walk through hell—telling you the unvarnished truth all the way—until something enduring emerges on the other side.

It's been a privilege to invest in, argue with, and learn from them across two decades of improbable survival.

—THOMAS GIESELMANN, CO-FOUNDER, HEADLINE

* * *

As college kids, Ali and Murti and friends showed up in my law office in 2005 with the idea of starting HotCampusParties as an online resource for college students to know where the best parties were going to be, extend invitations, and share with their friends. It quickly became clear that there would be no retainer in my future. The concept wasn't resonating with me, but I was immediately smitten by their enthusiasm, energy, and intelligence and had a sense that this was going to be an exciting and joyful experience.

My contribution of time and capital (in this and their future ventures) paid off in tangible return but, more significant to me, afforded me the privilege of getting to know them and marvel at the way they handled challenges and opportunities, their work ethic, and the value system that defined their business and personal conduct. Even as kids. Their taking me along on their wild ride was a wonderful gift for which I am forever grateful.

And how often does one get to see "KFC" listed as an expense item on a business plan?

—MARK GOLD, OF COUNSEL, SMITH GREEN & HOLMES, LLP

* * *

Two things come to mind from our first project—SuperMega-Fan (SMF).

I had big ambitions. I wanted SMF to be perfect, and when users did not adopt what we built, there were two key moments created by you, Ali. Each became a core memory.

First, our first pivot on SMF, when it was clear that v1 was not going to work. Twitch streamers just did not transact in the marketplace no matter what we did.

I was upset. You were calm. And then I was twice as upset as to how calm you were about trying another angle. Why not persist here? We spent so much time on this. How can we just move on?

Second, you asked me to write down the truths. What do we actually know? What did we learn? What are the facts? What do we strongly believe about the user and the space? What are our strengths?

To this day I go back to making a simple list of ground truths when attacking a tough problem.

—GEORGE KURDIN, MONK, STREAMLABS,
MICROSOFT, MINECRAFT

* * *

Since the beginning of my career in 2007, I've mostly worked with companies founded by Ali and Murti. It all started with Peanut Labs in 2007–2008, and later with Streamlabs, which was acquired by Logitech in 2019. When I moved to the US in 2013, the company had just $300,000 in the bank, and we began working on what we considered our final shot. Ali was handling partnerships, Murti was the front end, while I took care of the rest of the tech stuff. We were coding 12 hours a day and had a working product ready in just a few days—not months. Ali and Murti were incredible product owners—deeply in tune with user needs, fast decision makers, and always pushing for simplicity, speed, and impact. Their clarity of vision and obsession with product quality shaped everything we built.

After raising $16 million in venture capital, our team quickly grew from three to 100 people. Between 2013 and 2019, there were multiple moments when the company could have failed, but Ali and Murti always found a way—not just to survive but to grow exponentially. That drive is still there. I had a great time working with them. It was one of the most intense, rewarding, and inspiring periods of my career. Even after multiple successful exits, they're still chasing new ideas.

—SALMAN ALI, CTO, STREAMLABS

* * *

Every time I think of Ali and Murti, a few scenes come roaring back as vividly as yesterday.

It was late 2008. Shikha and I were working out of a coffee shop near Pacific Beach in San Diego when Ali called out of the blue to invite us to a Peanut Labs event in San Francisco. He was warm, disarming, and, true to form, immediately helpful. We were toying with moving north, and he offered introductions before we'd even packed a box. When we finally landed in San Francisco in early 2009, Ali was among the first to welcome us, and he already had more gatherings lined up.

At those events, Ali and Murti seemed to sit at the hub of the entire Facebook apps ecosystem: introducing founders to VCs, game designers to publishers, and somehow remembering everyone's backstory. Their parties had the best energy and the best rooms: Bubble Champagne Lounge nights that spilled into after-parties at their Embarcadero apartment with no defined end time. Ali would wander through with water in his own shot glass while topping off everyone else's tequila—the hospitality was real, and so was the mischievous grin.

My favorite? The Pirate Cruise. They booked an entire ship on the San Francisco Bay for four hours, raised a giant pirate flag, and told everyone to come dressed as pirates. It was glee-fully absurd and strategically brilliant. The boat was full of founders who ran massive online audiences, shoulder-to-shoul-der with Peanut Labs's sales team. After a few hours of dancing and drinking, people walked off that ship ready to do business. I know because we did, too, bringing our 21-million-user audi-ence to the table. That is Ali and Murti's signature: creativity and fun as a force multiplier for execution.

But it wasn't all parties. That same year they pulled us into their Christmas toy drive. The brothers were as quick to rally resources for a cause as they were to fill a dance floor. Over countless late nights swapping immigrant-founder stories, our friendship deepened. To this day, a startling share of my San Francisco network traces back to their generous introductions.

Another snapshot: movie night at their apartment with "Pirates of Silicon Valley." The credits roll, and it's 11:00 p.m. Most people would call it a night. Not these two. "Let's go to the office and brainstorm something world-changing," they said. We walked a block to a whiteboard-covered, hacker-es-que space, where Murti fired the opening question: "What's the most daring effing world-changing idea we can think of?" And then we went to work. If you think today's 9-9-6 culture is intense, theirs ran 7:00 a.m. to midnight, seven days a week, for years.

Murti, famously, never says no to a meeting. He just offers a

6:30 a.m. slot in your time zone. It's a quiet filter for hunger and grit. Show up, and you've already answered the first question.

This book captures that spirit: the audacity to make business joyful, the discipline to make joy productive, and the generosity to make both contagious. As you read, don't be surprised if you find yourself plotting a bold idea, texting a new friend, or penciling in a very early meeting. That's the Ali and Murti effect. Arrive for the fun, leave ready to build.

—ANAND AND SHIKHA CHHATPAR, TECH
ENTREPRENEURS, GROWTHCHAMP

* * *

One day, I met Ali for a game of tennis. He had just pulled off something remarkable—raising millions of dollars in a single event. The energy around him was electric, the kind of momentum most founders dream of. Six months later, everything had changed. The market had shifted, the path forward was murkier, and what once looked like a clear victory now required a full reset.

What struck me wasn't the setback itself but Ali's response. He wasn't shaken, defensive, or bitter. Instead, he accepted the new reality with a kind of calm clarity—as if the pivot was simply the next chapter waiting to be written. There was even a wry smile on his face, the smile of someone who knows that reinvention isn't failure but freedom. That moment has stayed with me, because it captures the essence of Ali's journey: grounded, resilient, and always ready to explore what's next.

—KEVIN CHOU, KABAM, SUPERLAYER, BRIGHTSAVER

* * *

Every once in a while, you meet someone who doesn't just survive chaos—they build a home inside it. Ali is one of those rare humans.

In 17 years of building startups, advising and investing in over 100 companies, I don't know if I've ever seen someone so comfortable in the chaos, so comfortable with discomfort, so capable in turning volatility into momentum. Most people cling to control; Ali doesn't. It's not blind optimism or reckless energy. It's a grounded kind of clarity, the sort that turns impossible odds into Tuesday morning work, because he knows a simple truth: when one's work is aligned with their nature, success is inevitable.

Resilience comes in many forms. Some fueled by ego, some by fear, some by necessity. But Ali's is different.

It's a unique fusion of stubbornness and flexibility, a refusal to quit married to the humility to change. Most founders bend the truth to fit their ambition; Ali uniquely and continuously bends himself to find it. The result is a kind of hard-won stillness when you interact with him. The kind that can only be earned by being broken and rebuilt, again and again, while gaining ground.

This book isn't about grit as a buzzword or perseverance as some kind of anecdote. It's about what it really looks like to keep showing up through the false starts, the internal and external doubt, the existential fear, the taste of failure that never quite leaves your mouth. It's not self-help either. It's field notes from someone who's lived in the arena and two decades in, still found meaning in each day within it. Ali also doesn't write like a guru. He writes like a survivor who's still curious, still building, still learning to find beauty in the wreckage. That's what makes this worth reading. Not because it tells you how to win but because it reminds you how to keep going when you are not.

—JAMES BESHARA, MAGIC MIND, TILT, AIRBNB,
Y COMBINATOR, ANGEL INVESTOR

$$\ast \ast \ast$$

When I first joined Streamlabs, the company had just gone through a difficult transformation. An unexpected pivot had shaken the team, forcing hard decisions and leaving behind a sense of loss. The air carried both the weight of what had changed and the spark of what could still be rebuilt. Despite the uncertainty, Ali and Murti's determination was what held everyone together, their focus and energy gave the team a sense of direction and belief that we could create something meaningful again. That mindset set the tone for everything that followed.

Months later, as we were developing Streamlabs OBS, we faced another moment of truth. The project was behind schedule, by a lot, and the pressure to deliver was intense. Shutting it down might have seemed like the practical choice. But again, Ali and Murti refused to give up. They believed in the vision and in the team's ability to make it happen. That belief made all the difference. When we finally launched SLOBS, it became a huge success, not just for us as builders but for millions of creators whose lives it helped transform.

Looking back, those moments remind me that great products don't just emerge from innovation alone; they're built on conviction, persistence, and a shared sense of purpose. That spirit is what made Streamlabs special, and what I'll always remember most.

—EDDY GHARBI, LEAD ENGINEER, STREAMLABS OBS

$$\ast \ast \ast$$

I first met Ali and Murti at a boat party full of inebriated Silicon Valley geeks determined to spend the evening embarrassing themselves. Amid the chaos, the two stood out as probably the only people on the boat that would wake without regrets. They were welcoming and politely indulged my obsession with gaming mechanics and user psychology—topics I bored way too many people with at the time.

As the years passed and we had more chances to spend time together, I always walked away from our conversations with insights that helped me grow as an entrepreneur. Pivoting a company can appear chaotic from the outside—but they are quietly intense and methodical in their approach to building businesses.

I'm thrilled that Ali and Murti wrote a book. I hope you enjoy it, and I know that you'll get a chance to laugh as well as learn from some of the hardest working and most insightful entrepreneurs I'm lucky to have met.

—BLAKE COMMAGERE, ENTREPRENEUR, ANGEL INVESTOR

* * *

Back in 2008–2009, roughly the peak of the Facebook Platform era, I received an email from Ali asking me to join him and Peanut Labs for a meetup. Even though I ran some Facebook applications with over 150 million users over their lifetime, I had no exposure to the vast community of risk-taking nerds and die-hards that I was about to meet in San Francisco.

Ali and Murti have a tendency to seek and attract brilliant, yet humble, folks, any place or time. Perhaps misery loves company, but so does success. The community that gravitated toward Ali and Murti has seen some of the brightest stars from the Silicon Valley, but you wouldn't have known it back then. Optimism will not fade from Ali and Murti even if a meteor hurtles toward them. That is a contagious thing, and perhaps a few of their sparks might land on you, the reader, igniting you for your own journey ahead.

—ATIF NAZIR, ENTREPRENEUR & FOUNDER

* * *

I've known Ali and Murti for the last five years, and every conversation with them has been a source of energy for me. They are among the humblest yet most supportive entrepreneurs I've come across. What I admire most is how open they are in sharing their own journeys—stories from the early days of building, lessons from handling the ups and downs, and the courage it takes to reset or pivot at the right time. Most founders struggle to let go of what they've built, but Ali and Murti have this rare wisdom of knowing when to move on and how to chase new opportunities with clarity and first principles.

For me, they have always been more than friends. They've been guides I turn to whenever I feel stuck. Whether it's about building culture, managing a team, setting up a board, or handling the tricky parts of investor communication, I've found myself leaning on their words and their experiences. They carry with them a whole library of learning about building companies, and I feel truly lucky to have had their presence in my journey.

—MISBAH ASHRAF, FOUNDER, JAR APP

* * *

I was introduced to Murti and Ali through a longtime friend and co-investor. He said, "I have this interesting company founded by two Pakistani brothers that look nothing like each other. They are smart, scrappy, and a lot of fun. You will love their story."

Murti and Ali were creative, imaginative, bold, and willing to experiment to survive. Their pivot from Xuqa to Peanut Labs was brilliant, creative, and born of necessity. It had to work; otherwise, the company was dead.

Their superpower is the ability to honestly assess whether or not things are working. Be like a scientist: have a thesis, test the thesis with an experiment, and then move on to the next test/thesis. First, you need to fully commit to a project and then periodically evaluate progress. Making adjustments as needed to pivot or, if necessary, wholesale restart the business. Their business career has demonstrated this feedback loop.

They have applied this approach to each of their startups. Stonks is another run of the same playbook: find a market need, test the thesis, iterate on the product, and see if the fish bite. If not, adapt. This is similar to the Marines learning cycle called Improvise, Adapt, and Overcome.

—ROBERT SIMON, BDC, ARIVA PARTNERS

* * *

I've watched Ali and Murti die three times.

Not literally, though there were moments when the weight they carried seemed almost unbearable. I'm talking about the death of dreams. The kind where you pour everything into something, watch it fail, and have to decide whether to stay down or get back up. Most people don't get back up. They can't.

The first failure breaks something fundamental in all of us, and we pivot into safer waters—a corporate job, a "realistic" path, something with a predictable trajectory that won't shatter us again. Ali and Murti have come back from the dead 40-plus times.

I had a front-row seat to this odyssey at Stonks.com. I watched them build a startup investment platform with a genuine belief it would democratize investing. When that didn't work, they didn't make excuses or blame the market. They listened, learned, and rebuilt it as a pre-IPO equity purchase platform. Then as a generational wealth for kids platform. Then as a tax optimization tool for creators. Each pivot wasn't a retreat—it was a calculated advance toward solving a real problem.

What they taught me about pivoting is magical: It's not about changing your mind. It's about keeping your promise to yourself that you will succeed, even when the path to get there looks nothing like what you imagined.

This book isn't a manual for building startups. It's a manual for building yourself into the kind of person who can't be stopped. The tactics will help you, sure. But what they are really teaching you is how to metabolize failure so completely that it becomes fuel instead of poison. By the time you're reading this, they might be on pivot 41. Or maybe Stonks became the rocket ship it was always meant to be. Either way, they'll still be standing, still building, still refusing to give up. They embody what Silicon Valley is all about—people who don't give up.

That's the lesson. Not that they succeeded but that they made success inevitable by being relentless in their pursuit.

—KUSHAGRA SHRIVASTAVA, CHRIS FONG, XOOGLER, KEY AI

* * *

It's a privilege to back talented founders even once. To do it again is truly special. At 500 Global, we've had the honor of backing Ali and Murti twice. Watching their journey has been nothing short of inspiring. From Streamlabs to Stonks, they've consistently shown what it means to build with speed, stay curious, and build with intention. With Stonks in particular, they immediately pulled us in as customers and testers. They were always eager for real feedback, no matter how candid, and would rapidly iterate. Their ability to pair velocity with depth and thoughtfulness has always stood out.

What I've always appreciated about Ali and Murti is their grounding in substance, trust, and working with good people. They don't buy into hype, nor do they chase signals. They tell it like it is. Beyond that, Ali makes time to help fellow founders and pay it forward. He and Murti truly embody 500's ethos and mission, and I remain deeply grateful that 500 has been part of their journey for the past 15 years.

—CHRISTINE TSAI, CEO, 500 GLOBAL

* * *

I'm lucky to have had a front-row seat to Ali and Murti doing exactly what this book is about: building and staying alive in a brutally hard space where the rules keep changing and most companies struggle to stay relevant. Creator tools and live streaming have had wave after wave of entrants, yet Stream-labs, in its many forms and evolutions, kept showing up with innovation for creators. We kept unlocking new capabilities, reacting to platform shifts, and we're still serving millions of creators years later. That is not luck. That is making pivoting a core competency and doing it with the kind of agility most teams lose as they get bigger. Even today, that culture runs through Streamlabs.

What always stood out to me was the way they worked. Talk to creators and actually live their problems. Listen to the market even when it's telling you something you do not want to hear. Ship something small today. Look at the real numbers tomorrow. Change course without ego. That rhythm is what kept Streamlabs growing while other companies were stuck in meetings. Pivoting is not failure. It's healthy chaos. It's how you keep your promise to users and earn the right to build the next thing. I saw them do it over and over.

—ASHRAY URS, HEAD OF STREAMLABS, LOGITECH

⋆ ⋆ ⋆

I had the unfortunate challenge of competing with Ali's company Streamlabs in the Twitch space. Ali and Murti are super scrappy. They hit millions of users, grew the business, and successfully sold it to Logitech. I was impressed.

This book captures their story, riding the big wave of livestreaming, and how they managed to build a successful company in the middle of a storm.

—SHAAN PURI, MFM, MILK ROAD, TWITCH

INTRODUCTION

When the email came through, I (Murti) was sitting in a hot tub in Vegas with my good friend Jaz, eight or 10 drinks in, feeling on top of the world. It was 2007; I was 21 and celebrating the sale of the company I'd started two years earlier with my brother, Ali. We had a signed purchase agreement. One million dollars was set to be wired the next day.

I always had my laptop with me, so it was sitting on the side of the hot tub when I heard the notification and then read the email from the buyers: "We've just had a board meeting and decided not to go through with the sale. Call me when you can."

I have never sobered up so quickly in my life.

Those were the early years of online social networking platforms. Our website, Xuqa.com, was the number one social network in Turkey at that time, with more users in Turkey than Facebook. My brother, Ali; our CTO, Prosper; and I had spent three years building it. We had close to 10 million users.

We'd spoken to multiple buyers, including MTV Viacom, and we'd accepted an offer from a Russian investing group. It had taken six months to negotiate the deal. We'd just spent a month in the grinder—handing over every number, every document, every analytics report, every contract, the full stack. Classic PITA due diligence. Ali and I were already working on our next pivot, and the proceeds from the sale of Xuqa were supposed to pay the salaries of our 20 employees while we got this next product off the ground.

We had two weeks of payroll left in the bank.

It was scary AF.

Just 24 hours earlier, the buyer had assured us they were excited to close the deal and were about to wire funds. And now, the deal was dead. In 14 days we wouldn't have money to pay any salaries or expenses. Our baby, our first real startup, would run out of cash and die. Our team had no freakin' idea.

I went from drunk to extremely focused in an instant, and my first thought was, *Fuck it. Time to go put it all on black*. In that moment, I figured there was no other way we'd survive. We could never figure out how to make enough money to survive in two weeks. Even with a signed purchase agreement, we had no way to legally enforce it against a Russian company. But maybe, just maybe, if I put everything in the bank on black at the roulette table and doubled or tripled the money, there would be enough time to figure it out.

I nearly did it.

Later in my life, I learned that the founder of FedEx had had the same experience. FedEx was days away from running out of cash. He was in Vegas. He actually *did* put it all on black, and he won. Maybe there were more balls on that guy than me; maybe I was too drunk to figure out whether the ATM would let me withdraw that much money. But in that moment, at 10:00 or 11:00 at night, instead of hitting the casino of that shitty motel, I got in my Honda Accord with Jaz, and we started driving.

We drove from Las Vegas to San Francisco through the night.

Jaz drove most of the way, and I slept a little. He got a speeding ticket somewhere on that 10- or 12-hour drive.

• • •

NO DEAL IS DONE UNTIL THE MONEY IS IN THE BANK.

• • •

Xuqa already had a VC (venture capitalist) who just a few months ago had almost killed us. Their advice: forget revenue, just chase users—they'd fund the rest. We didn't know better, so we did. We got 10 million users. Then the VC bailed. Said the space wasn't hot anymore, growth wasn't steep enough. They weren't going to rescue us.

With two weeks of cash, we were fighting for our lives.

I do my best work when shit hits the fan. I'm able to focus in a way that's impossible for me when things are okay. Maybe I'm a wartime CEO. We reached San Francisco at seven or so in the morning, and I immediately started hustling on a presentation for a fundraising conference happening the next day.

From there Ali, Prosper, and I took several steps. Ali and Prosper were in Pakistan with our engineers, where they had to fire dozens of great people working on Xuqa. They planned the layoffs on Saturday, and on "bloody Monday," more than 20 people who had worked immensely hard lost their jobs. All three of us slashed our own salaries to $0. We cut anything and everything that wasn't absolutely essential, lowering expenses to a third of what they had been. Ali implemented new ways to charge users on Xuqa with "peanuts" to make some revenue quickly (more on that story involving groupie girls and nudes in Chapter 4).

Magically, some revenue started to trickle in. We had bought a few more months of time.

I started fundraising very aggressively. I pitched more than 100 VCs in the next six months, getting turned down by almost every single one. Imagine what that many meetings ending in rejection does to your self-confidence: the smartest people in the world (or so I thought at the time) thought my company sucked. I spent those months driving up and down Highway 280 to Sand Hill Road, getting one rejection after the other. Then we found one VC, Pete Sinclair at Leapfrog Ventures, who took a chance on us. One yes, from more than 100 rejections.

We would have enough cash to survive. To pay our remaining team. And not immediately go out of business. To give our next pivot enough time to be born.

• • •

HUNDREDS OF REJECTIONS TO GET TO ONE TERM SHEET IS THE TYPICAL VC PROCESS FOR FIRST-TIME FOUNDERS.

• • •

We went on to raise $4.5 million to fund that next pivot before we sold the company for $30 million years later.

In a way, all our startup journeys were like those days after Vegas when we took a two-week runway, turned it into six months, and somehow found a way to get to product-market fit (PMF). They've never been linear or predictable. And they only looked successful in hindsight.

In the trenches, on most days, it felt like failing, like drowning.

WHY THIS BOOK

Today, in addition to working on our third startup, we've invested directly in 100 startups and a dozen VC funds, and we've mentored hundreds of new startup founders. The most common question we get asked is "Should I continue with what I'm doing, even if it's not working? Should I pivot or persevere?"

We're writing this book to share our stories on how we answered that big question. Forty times over.

You can't write a how-to guide for startups, so we're not going to try. Think about finance: People have tried for years to publish an investing philosophy or formula. Sometimes it works for a while, but then it stops working. To write and follow a how-to guide, the market would have to remain static, but it never does. Sometimes there are principles, but everything changes for startups every few years. By their very nature, startups are designed to grow very fast, as Paul Graham says. They are the Olympics of business, according to Shaan Puri. Anyone with a formula that tries to predict the future will always fall flat on their face.

Instead of a how-to, we're sharing our stories and observations, trusting that you'll find what's helpful to you. Rather than a definitive guide, we're offering something we've always needed more of: inspiration.

This book is for startup founders, startup investors, and anyone thinking about becoming a founder or working at an early-stage technology startup.

We get a kind of therapy from learning about other people's crazy, winding journeys, especially the parts where they get punched in the face. If you're reading this, we're guessing you do too. We want to show you what it's really like—it's not linear, not predictable, not all gold dust and rainbows. As Elon Musk describes it (quoting a friend), most days it really feels "like chewing glass and staring into the abyss."[1]

Every startup goes through dark days. It will happen to you. Even if you come from VP roles at Meta or Google with a computer science degree from Stanford and millions in VC funding, you will throw up in the middle of the night. You will lose friends. Your girlfriend or spouse may leave you. You will have health issues. You may go broke and lose the house. And you will wait 8 to 10 years to know if you were even right.

You need to go in prepared, knowing the challenges you face will be incredibly tough but also knowing you're not alone.

This shit is hard. You're going to fail much more than you succeed. No one is going to understand what you are going through—not your wife or husband, not your employees, and least of all your therapist. You're going to live through some crazy stories of your own. But that's what makes it fun. This is an incredible experience. Don't give up; keep going.

People talk about the wins. Strategies to scale. The big mergers and acquisitions and funding rounds. Nobody talks about the dark days. Shit hitting the fan will be most of your days. Ninety-five days out of 100 will be gut-wrenchingly bad. Nobody tells you this before you start. We will.

This book is a collection of real stories. Stories that will entertain, teach a little, and give you some hope. Show you it's hard and how we got through it.

Share our energy. So that you don't give up. So that you know that you are *not* alone. So that you might make it.

JUST KEEP SWIMMING

Dr. Richter and his team at Johns Hopkins in the 1950s did an interesting social experiment on mice. They put the mice in water and measured the time they could swim before they gave up and drowned. It was about five minutes.

Then they repeated the same experiment, except that right at minute five, when the mice were about to give up, the experimenters rescued them. Later they put the rescued mice in the water again, and those little fuckers went on for *six hours. Six hours!* Because this time they believed that if they hung on a little bit more, they'd make it.

Being a startup founder is like that. If you can make it a little farther, pivot once or twice more, you'll make it.

You won't drown unless you stop swimming.

→ CHAPTER 1 ←

GROWING UP IN PAKISTAN

Ali: My first business was selling handmade stickers to kids in first grade. I drew trees, houses, and toys on blank sticker sheets. I colored them with markers, cut them out, and sold them to my class for 1 Rupee (~ $0.03 at the time). Pure kid economics.

By second grade, I leveled up. Transformers cards were the rage, like Pokémon now. Everyone was trading. I did too. But trading has risk. Why risk getting stuck with junk when you could just arbitrage? I saw stores with giant boxes of card packs. Got curious—where did *they* get them? I asked around, found the wholesale market, and convinced my mom to take me. I bought packs for 70 cents, then sold them at school for a dollar. No trading, just clean markup.

Soon my friends wanted in. I handed them packs, they sold to their friends, and we had a little resale empire. I'd bring 10 to 20 packs a week, and they moved them. Eventually the principal found out, called all my reseller friends into her office, and said, "You can't have a business in second grade," and shut the whole thing down. Regulators suck, man.

GLUING THE PIECES

Ali and Murti, growing up in Pakistan

Our dad ran corporate workshops and training. Most of our childhood, he struggled. But he kept at it. Eventually, he broke through—he's now the Tony Robbins of the Middle East. Watching him on stage makes business feel exciting.

Our mother always told us in no uncertain terms that we were poor and had to work really hard to be someone; there was no other way. Our father would drop us off at school on his motorbike (yes, in developing countries entire families can fit on a motorbike). Mom picked us up in her little beat-up Suzuki FX and carted us to extracurricular and after-school activities. She was a tiger mom and pushed us hard so that we could escape. We owe her for that.

Ali: But at home, things were rough. Our parents fought. Loudly. Constantly. Sometimes it got physical. I remember Mom banging her head on a wall during a fight. I was six. Dad would disappear for days. Think of what that does to a kid. As the older sibling, I think their fighting affected me more than Murti. I felt like I was responsible and had to shield him, that at some level, this was all my fault (it wasn't, of course, but try explaining that to a six-year-old). I still carry some of this guilt today.

They say that all parents damage their kids when raising them—some leave scratches, others shatter. Our parents shattered.

We lived in a joint family house—one room per family, cousins everywhere. That part was fun. But the fighting spilled out. Everyone blamed our mother. She in turn made us believe that she was being unfairly victimized, that Dad was cheating, and everyone was torturing her. We believed her. We were kids. Eventually our family moved out.

In high school, there was a big argument. Dad grabbed a belt. We stood between him and Mom. He couldn't get through. So he went to the closet, pulled out a loaded gun, pointed it at my head. Held it there. I thought, *Okay, shoot if you want, but you're not going to harm our mother.*

That day the police came. Our parents eventually divorced.

Our father stopped supporting us financially when we went to college. Our mother didn't work. We were broke. We knew that nothing and no one was going to save us. We had to find ways to make money and support her and ourselves. There was no family trust fund; there was no father; there was no backup plan. That pressure is what pushed us to start building.

Many years later, I discovered that my mom suffered from a severe personality disorder. On Reddit I found a survivor community of family members who had loved ones who behaved just like my mom—horror stories of abuse, control, victimhood, and lies. People suffering from this disorder entirely believe the made-up things they say. They are socially high-functioning;

no one sees anything different unless they live with them for an extended time. Talking to the other survivors, I realized, "Holy shit, this is exactly my entire life." All the symptoms matched. We had been walking on eggshells around her all this time.

It took 30 years to realize what was happening. Healing will likely take the rest of our lives.

Our father, while no saint, was nowhere near as bad as our mother had made him out to be. He has flaws but was simply trying to cope while struggling to get his own business off the ground. It wasn't until many years later, after I got married and saw my wife's family up close, that I realized how loving and nurturing a regular family can be. I saw what "normal" looked like. Even now, it moves me to tears.

We've spent a lot of time healing these broken relationships with our father, and with estranged uncles, aunts, and cousins. We're learning how to manage our mother with her condition. It feels like Murti and I have grown up as orphans, in a world where we've only had each other to rely on.

A lot of entrepreneurs come from troubled childhoods in some way: poverty, broken families, abuse, orphans, the death of a parent. This kind of trauma can either break you or make you, and we were super lucky that we had each other as a support system–being close in age, sharing this trauma together, being young when the internet was booming, and ending up at the same college together. We were lucky we survived and thrived; many don't.

Sometimes we wonder: If we didn't have so many struggles in our family situation, would we have had the fortitude to go through our startup journey? Could we have made so many pivots and survived the ups and downs? Maybe we had to build the mental endurance, the capacity for suffering. Maybe all this family suffering was training in disguise.

DIAL-UP MODEMS AND WEBSITES

Murti: We were teenagers, around 13 and 15, in 1999, when the internet started booming and Pakistan got dial-up. I took a website design course one summer and learned to make websites in HTML.

All the local business owners were old people who couldn't even operate a computer, let alone build a website. They'd make a website by scanning their physical brochure and uploading it as an image. The site was one image that took five minutes to load, inch by inch. Naturally, the next thing was to make websites for local brands. We partnered up with a couple friends (shout-out to co-founder Zaki) and went around town making websites. Everyone in Pakistan plays cricket, and in Karachi, there are no fields or stadiums. People played in the street. So we pitched Nike on a street cricket website and built and released it. We built a website for Pakola, the largest soft drink manufacturer in Pakistan, and one for Pakistan's largest tea distributor.

We called the business Gaming Ventura. Over three summer vacations, we scaled it to 15 employees. We made decent money—enough to rent some terrible office space and pay the people who worked for us every summer. That office had a hole in the wall, a broken bathroom, and we had to fix all the shit ourselves. The elevator was so bad that it fell with one of our guys in it, and the poor guy broke a leg. The whole building really should have been condemned.

The website business looked great on college essays; it showed initiative and uniqueness. We also participated in many extracurriculars, including rifle shooting, other sports, debate, and the Science Olympiad. We were trying, as international students, to not only get into top US colleges; we needed them to pay for everything too. The full scholarship was almost more important than the college. If you run the math, that is around 100-times harder than just getting into Harvard.

Our business and extracurriculars worked: When I was 16, I went to Atlantic College in Wales to finish up high school on scholarship, and Ali went to Williams College in Massachusetts on a scholarship of his own. Our schools even paid for our food, room and board, and annual flights home! (Ali: Fun fact. Murti and I sometimes get asked why our last names are different, even though we are brothers. Nothing exciting here—I filled out my passport form incorrectly when making my first passport 30 years ago. It stuck as I immigrated to the US for college. Now it's nearly impossible to go fix the entire paper trail.)

Every summer we'd go back home to Pakistan and start the website business again. It would be great for two or three months, and then we'd go back to school and put it on pause. We also started a college counseling business while we lived in Pakistan, hosting workshops on applying to colleges abroad for a few hundred people at a time. We'd book out a conference room at a hotel for kids to come to a day-long primer on colleges in the US, UK, and Canada. What are the top colleges? Who has the most money to give out in scholarships? What do they look for? What test scores do you need? It just made sense to turn our college admissions success into another business.

I paid for food at Atlantic College in Wales selling cigarettes. British food is so fucking shit that I lost weight and was sick all the time. But I couldn't bring myself to eat the food. Words cannot describe how bad not only British food is but especially at this boarding school. So cigarettes kept me alive—I bought a pack for $0.50 in Pakistan and resold them illegally for $3.50. Used the profit to order kebabs. Rinse and repeat.

Later, we both decided to drop out of college. Part of me was just waiting to get life started, and I couldn't see the value in spending four years on theoretical bullshit when I needed money to live. Especially with our father not supporting us anymore. Starting a business felt like a great way to get life going. Now I look back and think it would be amazing to go spend four years just learning something for the fun of it. But back then, the mindset was *I've gotta survive.*

PURPOSE

Ali: In the first years of Gaming Ventura, we both had similar dreams at nearly the same time. In Murti's dream, we built a large tech company making websites and outsourcing other tech stuff. We used the money to start a university, teach, and do a lot of good in the world. I was in an accounting internship, so my dream was about starting an accounting firm, but I did the same thing with the money I earned in the dream.

When boys and girls hit puberty in the Muslim Shia tradition, they go through the *misaaq*: a ceremony where they pledge to do good, pray, be honorable, and be charitable, similar to a bar mitzvah. After I had my misaaq, two men I didn't know came up to me at the ceremony. They were clothed in white robes and asked to see my hand. I was stunned as to why someone would ask this from a stranger, but without hesitation I offered them my hand. After looking at it closely and examining the lines on my hand, they said, "You'll be given great wealth. Do not keep it to yourself. Let it flow. Pass it on. Let it flow." At that time we were broke; we were nobody.

Years later, I saw those two men in a dream I had while in college. They had a different message for me (we're saving that for our next book). I have never been happier in my life as I was after that dream. Perhaps that will be a sequel to this book someday.

Twenty years later, after we sold Streamlabs, we donated most of what we made to charity as we had both pledged. As part of that, we started a 501(c)(3) nonprofit called Pledges to teach coding to kids in developing countries. As of now, over 20,000 students from various developing countries have learned to code for free (or deferred payment) through Pledges. You can view real time stats on our website: pledges.com.

We think everyone is on a path, and if you look closely enough and listen carefully enough, you'll find signs early on. The signs tell you where you're going, what challenges you'll face, and what you've been sent here to overcome.

You cannot go far without knowing why you're going.

Find yours.

• • •

"THE MOST BEAUTIFUL PEOPLE WE HAVE KNOWN ARE THOSE WHO HAVE KNOWN DEFEAT, KNOWN SUFFERING, KNOWN STRUGGLE, KNOWN LOSS, AND HAVE FOUND THEIR WAY OUT OF THE DEPTHS. THESE PERSONS HAVE AN APPRECIATION, A SENSITIVITY, AND AN UNDERSTANDING OF LIFE THAT FILLS THEM WITH COMPASSION, GENTLENESS, AND A DEEP LOVING CONCERN. BEAUTIFUL PEOPLE DO NOT JUST HAPPEN."

—ELISABETH KÜBLER-ROSS

• • •

CHAPTER 2

HACKING COLLEGE

Murti: By chance, two years after Ali, I also got into Williams College on a full ride. The summer before I left for Williams, Gaming Ventura was flourishing. We'd fixed up that crappy building and added its first air conditioning, a water machine, and computers for our 20 or so employees. Since we both had to leave, we hired a friend of Ali's to manage the office. "Mariam" seemed competent enough to take on the task of keeping everything running.

The office that routinely flooded, had holes in the walls, and had an elevator fall. Should've been condemned.

At freshman induction, I decided to go on a three-day hike with my new classmates. Of course, since we were supposed to be bonding and adventuring, we had no internet, no phone, no computers.

When I got back, Gaming Ventura was gone.

The manager we'd hired had quit within days of starting. A client had been unhappy with the service and canceled their project, and Mariam wasn't prepared to take responsibility for the business. She didn't fight to keep the client or do what needed to be done to find a new client. She just left.

Without a manager to fix the crisis, everyone else quietly quit too. Since we were in America, there wasn't much we could do short of flying back to try and salvage the situation. After years of building this business, it fell apart within a week.

In retrospect, it's clear that Mariam had nine-to-five energy, not founder energy. If Ali and I lost a client, we'd do everything to get them back or find new clients. We expected her to go do some sales, win the client back, do something to make it work, or find new projects. But she didn't, and neither did anyone else on the team.

So we were back to fucking zero.

• • •

**STARTUPS ARE LIKE SHARKS. IF THEY
STOP SWIMMING, THEY DIE.**

• • •

Every startup has to find a way to keep pushing, keep moving, keep carrying forward momentum, even when things fall apart. This comes from the founders' energy—the momentum, optimism, and relentless action founders bring to their endeavors. Founder energy is the greatest force in the startup (business) world, and there is no substitute. As founders, you, and you alone, are responsible for moving your startup or business forward.

Like sharks, if you stop moving, you'll sink and die.

COLLEGE TINKERING

Ali: In my first two years at college before Murti arrived, I made money in a couple of different ways. One of them was selling DVDs. I'd get illegal DVDs in Pakistan for 10 cents a piece, load up a suitcase, and bring them back to sell for 20 bucks. Of course, US Customs was a problem. To get around that, I took all the DVDs out of the boxes, put them in a CD case, and pretended they were music. Customer care was also an issue: often, the DVDs didn't work. So I brought two or three of the same movie, just in case a DVD didn't work and needed replacing. Doing a refund was far more expensive than a simple exchange.

Later I built a college website called EphBay. eBay existed then, but shipping was such a pain that I thought we should have a local option that didn't require shipping. College students, in particular, are within walking distance of hundreds or thousands of other students who need similar things: books, dorm room furniture, computers, sports equipment. The density allowed a local market to exist without the need for shipping, at least for things students wanted or needed.

A couple of friends and a developer in Pakistan worked with me on the site. I remember friends being over the moon about what they'd bought, like my roommate who got an Apple computer from a professor for a grand total of ONE dollar (shout-out to Jonathan and Colin, college buddies who helped with EphBay). Running EphBay was fun, but it never got big enough to make money. Keeping it going required constant energy, especially the marketing: flyers around campus, getting someone with a mailing list to give us a shout-out. Once I lost momentum, the marketplace transactions dried up.

Once Murti joined me at Williams, we looked for other ways to make money. We knew we wanted to build a startup. We didn't know what it would look like, but we knew it would involve the internet. So we needed servers to start messing around.

But we needed money to buy our first servers. Williams College was generous with our scholarships—a foreign concept to us. In Pakistan, the culture around us was aggressive: everyone undercutting and cheating everyone else. Getting to New England and seeing people treat each other with generosity was a welcome surprise. It helped us feel that America was the greatest country on Earth, welcoming to immigrants, and that the American dream was alive and well.

Our scholarships included meal plans. So, we decided to go off the meal plans, get the $800 cash, and use that to buy our servers. Every day for a year we'd buy a five-dollar footlong from Subway and eat half for lunch, half for dinner. You've heard of ramen-profitable; this was startup funding from Subway footlong sandwiches (Subway: we're open to sponsorships).

. . .

**IT IS CALORICALLY POSSIBLE TO LIVE ON
SUBWAY FIVE-DOLLAR FOOTLONG SANDWICHES
IF YOU EAT HALF FOR LUNCH, AND HALF FOR
DINNER. AT LEAST WHEN YOU'RE 19.**

. . .

Murti: Once we had the servers, we still needed internet bandwidth. We could have used our dorm room ethernet connections, but we didn't want college IT to notice if we were using a thousand times more bandwidth than everyone else. So we put the servers in the IT lab where I worked, which was unmetered.

Nobody at Williams College was doing anything entrepreneurial back then. The school produced doctors, investment bankers, consultants, and a few liberal arts professors. The only notable tech entrepreneur that the college had produced was Bo Peabody, who founded Tripod back in the '90s.

As we got busier building this first startup, I looked for the easiest classes I could find in order to stay enrolled, keep my scholarship, and keep my student visa. I took Physics 101 with all the football players, and I didn't go to a single class except for the midterm and the final. Got an A.

Later I also took Oceanography. I got a D on that midterm, and I had a Dean's Warning for it. Mathematically, I couldn't have ended up with an A in the class, but I did get an A on the final. I think my professor was so impressed with me trying to build a startup that she gave me an A for that.

. . .

COLLEGE IS A GREAT PLACE TO INCUBATE A STARTUP. YOUR FOOD AND HOUSING ARE BASICALLY PAID FOR, SO NO NEED TO RAISE MONEY EARLY, AND YOU HAVE A SEA OF POTENTIAL CO-FOUNDERS.

. . .

Ali: My junior year, I lived across the hall from Prosper, a computer-science major who was very good with women. Different ladies often came by his room and drew hearts and kisses on the whiteboard hanging on his door. I had to know this guy.

Ramadan fell in October that year, and I was fasting. Which was tough, since everyone was eating and drinking all day. At the end of the day at sunset, I grabbed a pizza and brought it back to my room. Prosper was outside his room, moping around. He looked hungry. I offered him a slice. He said thanks and went back to his room.

Years later he later told me that he was very impressed that someone who hadn't eaten all day would be willing to share their food. We became fast friends.

At the time, Murti and I were looking for a technical co-founder to help us build, since working with offshore talent in Pakistan was too difficult and cumbersome. Co-founders cannot be remote—things will take too long. Your early team must be in the same room as you.

Prosper was graduating from college and hadn't lined up a job yet. We offered him the co-founder role in the startup we were building, and he became our CTO.

. . .

REMOTE WORK DOES NOT WORK FOR EARLY-STAGE STARTUPS.

. . .

BEYOND BUSINESS PLANS AND CLASSES

While we were tinkering with the servers, we also thought about launching a peer-to-peer news network. Long before Trump and fake news, we were skeptical of news, especially in other countries prone to censorship. We thought governments would be unable to censor a LimeWire-style peer-to-peer news network, so we wrote a 40-page business plan about it. The plan went absolutely nowhere, because it was a dumb idea—no one wanted a peer-to-peer news network.

But we were doing the MBA thing, the stuff they say you should do in business classes. We thought we should write out long business plans and that this was a prerequisite to building. This was a classic example of whiteboarding, coming up with an ostensibly "smart" idea, then writing a long plan about it.

You should never do any of this—business classes, business plans, none of it.

In fact, the longer the business plan, the lower the probability your idea will work. That includes pitch decks. You don't need a 20- or 30-page PowerPoint. Write a one-page memo. A single slide. And only if you absolutely need to. We've raised over $50 million in venture capital across three startups, and the difference couldn't be more stark: no slides, lots of money; lots of slides, no money.

People who plan are usually those who don't have traction. No amount of presenting or polishing can substitute for customers, revenue, usage, or traction. If you focus on actually getting traction and building something in the real world—writing code, designing, calling people to make sales—that's far better than spending energy on hocus-pocus revenue models. I did a 10-year revenue model for the news network, and it looked fucking amazing! But there was no PMF, because there was no product–there was nothing.

Later in our careers, we saw the same relationship with board deck slides when we had a formal board for our startups. The better the business was doing, the fewer the slides, and the happier board members and investors were. They didn't even complain about the sandwiches. If the business was doing poorly, we'd make more slides to try and explain, which helped no one and made the situation worse. No amount of gourmet food helped here.

• • •

FOLLOW Y COMBINATOR'S ADVICE: ONE SLIDE ONLY FOR FUNDRAISING. EVERYONE ELSE IS WRONG. IF IT'S NOT WORKING, YOUR BUSINESS IS THE PROBLEM, NOT YOUR SLIDES.

• • •

In 2005, Steve Jobs made a famous commencement speech at Stanford about dropping out of classes for his business major and instead taking classes that interested him. One of these was a calligraphy class, which became the basis of the typography on every Mac computer.

We had a similar mindset. While at Williams College, neither of us took any business classes. The internet was so new. How could college classes teach us what we needed to know to launch an internet-related startup?

In case you missed it: no entrepreneur should ever take a business class. People who learn "business" are just learning how to manage others who do the real work. Instead, learn to do the real work. Learn a craft, skill, or technology that's useful. At an early-stage startup, you must know how to do the real work. There is no managing and scaling. As Paul Graham says, there are really only two roles at an early-stage startup: building or selling. Learn one of these.

Ali: I accidentally ended up in a class about Sufism (Islamic mysticism) my first year, and I loved it. I took more Sufi classes and got the religion department to invite different speakers. At one of them, the famous translator of Sufi poetry, Coleman Barks, came to read some poetry with a cello performance alongside. Timeless Sufi wisdom has helped me develop good taste in storytelling and writing. It also helped me develop a resilience practice with daily meditation that helped me get through difficult startup days (we'll talk about developing resilience practices later).

I also had a couple of friends who were into startups, and we started an entrepreneurship society at Williams. We held business plan competitions (yes, even though we don't think you should write one) and invited guest speakers to the school. My favorite speaker was the WorldCom CFO, who came and spoke to us after he got out of prison for an $11 billion accounting fraud. That was quite a story, a slippery slope that didn't start out as fraud but became fraud over time.

I've noticed that anyone who demonstrates the ability to make something happen that didn't exist before, who finds a way to get money and people together, to make things *happen*, could have the energy to become a founder. Entrepreneurship requires high agency.

Today we look for employees who have been busy organizing things, contributing to ambitious projects, or competing at a high-level. A good example is a self-taught developer or folks who contribute to open-source projects or compete in hackathons. They weren't drinking or skating through class; they were contributing to open-source projects or entering startup competitions or tinkering. We also like to hire athletes, particularly for sales. They've worked hard at something for a long period of time without giving up, and that's never easy.

SUCCESS IS HARMFUL

Ali: I was a straight-A kid through high school and my first year of college, and that turned out to be a handicap in startups. I had to unlearn perfectionism—the need to finish everything, to make the "right" decision, to feel like I was succeeding because the structure said so.

When we started building a startup at Williams, my grades fell from A's to C's. That was the first time I consciously chose failure. I had to let go of the idea that success meant getting everything right.

Straight-A students expect a predictable world: work hard, get rewarded. Pavlov rings the bell, you get the treat. But startups don't work like that. Hard work is table stakes. There's no guaranteed output for any amount of input.

The VP of HR at Netflix once gave a talk called "Silver Spoon." Netflix had analyzed years of data on employee performance and found two groups: those who came from privilege and those who were hungry. The hungry ones outperformed the silver spoons every single time.

Startups are the same way. They reward hunger, not pedigree. If you've been trained your whole life to expect a gold star for effort, the moment you don't get one, it messes with you.

In startups, you can do everything right for years—and get nothing. Then one day, everything changes at once. The rewards, when they come, are *asymmetric*. You're poor, you're poor, you're poor—and then suddenly you're rich.

Most people aren't built for that. Humans crave consistency—steady effort, steady reward. But startups are chaos.

That's why the people who succeed at big, structured companies often struggle in startups. The FAANG veteran used to bonuses and promotions every six months burns out fast. The desperate kid trying to prove something keeps going.

Two months before Twitch sold to Amazon for $1 billion, founders and early employees were trying to sell their shares for pennies. No one wanted them. There was no market, no clear reward signal. Then overnight, the company was worth a billion.

That's the truth about startups: there's no straight line between input and output, as we were about to find out.

...

IN STARTUPS, THERE'S NO DIRECT CORRELATION
BETWEEN INPUT AND OUTPUT. DON'T EXPECT
CONSISTENT REWARDS OR SMOOTH PROGRESS.

REWARDS, IF ANY, WILL BE RARE,
UNPREDICTABLE, AND WILDLY ASYMMETRIC.

...

→ CHAPTER 3 ←

STARTUPS WITH TERRIBLE NAMES: HOTCAMPUSPARTIES, IVENTSTER, XUQA

Our first true startup began when we walked into TD Bank in Williamstown, Massachusetts, and tried to open a bank account for HotCampusParties, Inc. We shit you not—the company that eventually sold for $30 million as Peanut Labs started its life as HotCampusParties, Inc. The bank manager looked at us as if we were a porn website, or something worse.

She eventually opened our bank account.

HotCampusParties was a website listing all the parties on campus. We printed out a few hundred flyers, posted them all over campus, and within a weekend a good chunk of the Williams student body was signed up. Our users would post parties happening at fraternities, at sorority houses, and in dorm rooms—or they'd get the latest on where to find these parties. It was going well–until Campus Security found out. Then they showed up at all the parties to bust people for under-age drinking.

So much for HotCampusParties.

Okay, we thought, *What if we just did events rather than parties?* Colleges have a lot of events, so we pivoted to a similar events site called iVentster focused on campus events.

This was 2005. Facebook had launched only a year earlier, and one way they'd grown was through a viral email invite system. Users could enter their Hotmail or Yahoo! Mail password, import all their contacts, and send them all a friend request via email. They also plugged into college LDAP (Lightweight Directory Access Protocol) servers to access available student email addresses. The email wasn't just an ad; it would say, "Ali has added you as a friend. Click to accept!" Then, of course, the invitee would have to join Facebook before they could accept.

We were able to use Facebook to implement a similar viral hack for iVenster. At that time any user could export a spreadsheet of all their friends' names and email addresses from Facebook (crazy, we know). So we built a tool that lets users download their social graph and easily invite all of their Facebook friends to the iVenster site via email.

That simple ability to share the site with a couple hundred people at once led to exponential growth. In a few days, we went from zero to 300,000 users. Suddenly, we had to learn all the basics of servers, database management, and optimizing systems for hundreds of thousands of users—stuff they don't teach you in college. Prosper was a computer science major, and even he'd learned none of this. We found information online, looked at what other people were doing, and traded notes with others who were building similar products, such as Michael Birch of Birthday Alarm (who would go on to start Bebo).

Murti: Now that we had so many users, this project was going to cost real money. It couldn't run off of one computer sitting in the college IT lab anymore. We needed to fundraise. I knew a lot of Williams College alumni were rich, so I found the college alumni directory and started cold emailing people. "Hi, my name is Murti," I'd write. "We're making a social networking site for students and getting some traction. Do you want to invest in our company?"

Mark and Ellen Gold, our very first angel investors

Over three or four weeks, I probably messaged a few thousand alumni, and a few replied. That's how Mark Gold, a lawyer in Williamstown, became our very first investor. He met with us, liked us, and wrote us a $25,000 check.

Mark also hosted a dinner at his house for us and invited a few friends and family so we could pitch them. His brother and friends put another $50,000 into the company. Mark is still the angel investor we think of most fondly, because he was the first. He took a chance on us as young kids and made an incredible difference in our lives.

Eventually, Mark paid off the mortgage on his house with

money he invested in iVentster (which eventually sold as Peanut Labs) and our second startup, Streamlabs. Good karma goes around.

Silicon Valley is made of this stuff. People taking a chance on kids with no track record.

Another Williams alum met with us after I emailed him, and he agreed to invest $50,000. He'd sent half of it and was planning to send the other half in another month or two. But the time came and went, and he wouldn't reply to our emails or phone calls. Eventually I got in touch with his wife, who told me he'd had a heart attack and died. "Oh my God!" I said. "But can you still send the money?"

She did, bless her.

• • •

FOR FIRST-TIME FOUNDERS, IT TYPICALLY TAKES CONTACTING HUNDREDS OF POTENTIAL INVESTORS TO GET YOUR FIRST CHECK.

• • •

IVENSTER

During spring break we stayed on campus while the rest of the students left. We were in the IT Lab at 1:00 a.m. with our co-founder, Prosper, while he was coding. We had been working all day, now well into the night. Finally he said, "Oh man, I'm done!" and collapsed, sleeping on the floor next to the desk.

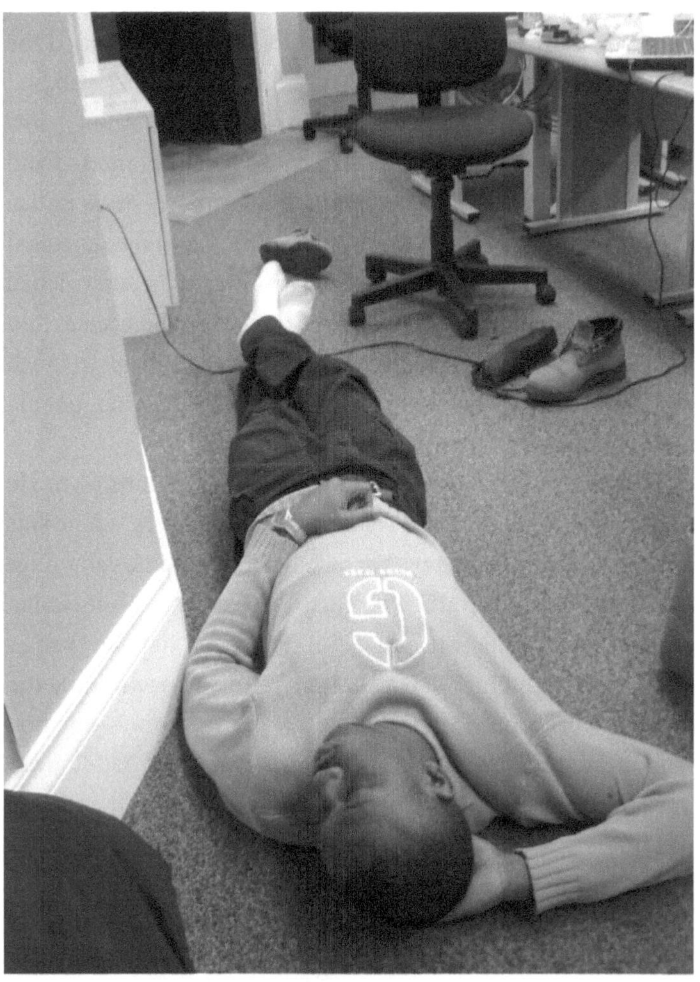

Prosper sleeping on the floor in the computer science lab

A few minutes later campus security came by, saw two brown guys and a black guy in the IT Lab when all the other students had left, and mistook us for homeless people. "What are you guys doing? Why are you sleeping here?" they asked us. They were going to arrest us and throw us out.

Thankfully we had our student IDs on us! We avoided the locker that night and promised not to sleep in the IT Lab.

Shortly after that eventful evening, BV Capital (now Headline)—a venture capital firm based in San Francisco and originally spun out of Bertelsmann in Germany—took notice of iVenster as it continued to go viral. BV Capital cold called the phone number attached to the iVenster domain and reached Prosper. He couldn't understand the thick German accent, told them to buzz off, and hung up. Somehow, they still got in touch with us. It was probably a lucky break, because when people say no to VCs, they just want to invest more.

The firm sent one of their associates to Williamstown. He told me years later that he wasn't expecting much, but he was impressed when he met us. We talked about lifetime value, cost of acquisition, and viral coefficients. Our plan was sophisticated enough that they flew us out to San Francisco to pitch them.

After the pitch, BV Capital and Tom Gieselmann, the partner who sponsored the deal, put up $300,000—our first institutional VC investors. The catch was that we had to drop out of college, move to San Francisco, and work on the startup full time.

"What's in San Francisco?" we asked.

"You just have to be here," they said.

We told someone in the college admin office that we were planning to drop out. The school president found out and called us into his office.

"Do not drop out," he told us. "You're making the worst mistake of your life."

He wanted us to enjoy the four years of college and go do our startup thing after that. Quitting school to start a business wasn't an accepted path at Williams College, and we were screwing up the school's near-perfect graduation rate.

"Fuck it," we decided when we talked later. "Let's do it." We told our parents we were dropping out of college, packed up, and moved to San Francisco. Our parents had a heart attack—both their kids, after winning scholarships to the number one undergrad college in America, had just decided to throw it all away. And for what? Some internet fad?

But we had only raised $300,000. With the average developer salary being around $150,000 in San Francisco, that money would only last four to six months. That just wasn't enough time or runway to build a startup.

Given we were from Pakistan, we knew how cheap it was there. Developer salaries averaged just $10,000 annually. So we packed up again and moved to Karachi, where that $300,000 would last more than 18 months and pay 15 employees.

Ten months after moving to Pakistan, we flew back to San Francisco for some meetings and caught up with our VCs. They were surprisingly happy and relieved to see us.

Relieved? What?

At coffee, one of the associates admitted, "We honestly thought two Pakistanis and a Nigerian [Prosper was from New York, but originally Nigerian] had taken our money and run away with it. So you guys coming back was a nice surprise."

LOL.

• • •

DO WHATEVER YOU CAN TO BE FRUGAL. THE MORE YOU CAN EXTEND YOUR STARTUP RUNWAY, THE MORE TIME AND SHOTS ON GOAL YOU'LL HAVE TO FIND SOMETHING THAT WORKS.

• • •

Then iVentster died.

The first version of iVentster spread fast. Too fast, maybe. It was a classic viral hack—quick to rise but just as quick to vanish. Most of our users were college students, and when summer hit, they disappeared. And they didn't come back. The product hadn't sunk deep enough into their habits. It solved a problem they had in the moment but one they forgot about over the summer.

Worse, by the time school started again, Facebook had quietly cloned us. They added events natively on Facebook, and our users had no reason to return.

We were a feature, not a platform, that Facebook had just copied.

The Lindy Effect, an unofficial law of the internet that's less famous than Moore's Law but just as accurate, states that the longer something has been around, the longer it's likely to continue being around.

Not great for viral startups.

Our rocket ship crashed nearly as fast as it started. We were back to starting from zero.

XUQA

When iVentster died, we'd just moved halfway across the world. Quitting wasn't even on the table. We knew we had to build something better—something users wouldn't abandon as soon as summer rolled around. The problem was obvious: the product had been a one-trick pony with poor retention. To survive, we needed something stickier. A network, not just a tool.

In 2005 Myspace and Friendster were the kings of social networking. Facebook was still small, still college-only. We decided to rebuild. Rebrand. We relaunched iVentster as a new social network called xuqa.com (mostly because Murti liked smoking the traditional hookah pipe, which rhymes with xuqa). Xuqa (pronounced *Zoo*-kah) would compete with Facebook for colleges.

But by the time we launched, Facebook had blocked the ability to export your friends' email addresses. RIP—our original viral growth hack was dead. We tried importing Gmail, Hotmail, Yahoo! contacts. It kind of worked but wasn't targeted. Still, we shipped fast, added features faster, and users came. Xuqa flew past 1 million users.

Then 5 million.

Then 10 million.

Those months were the most intense we've ever worked. We were in Pakistan, in a dusty office packed with fresh grads who were more like roommates than employees. It felt more like a hacker house than a company. Myspace sold to NewsCorp for $580 million. Bebo went to AOL for $850 million. Facebook was quietly on its way to an IPO and eventually becoming a $2 trillion behemoth. We barely noticed. We were too busy pulling all-nighters. The space was moving too fast.

The Xuqa office mural: handprinted by everyone who worked there.

No one had taught us how to do this. Not in school, not in life. We were running a high-traffic production system—probably one of the top 100 busiest in the US—out of a developing country with rolling blackouts. Built on free open-source (Linux, Apache, mySQL, pHp) because proprietary solutions were too expensive. AWS didn't exist. We ordered servers by email. If a disk failed or a cable came loose, you handled it. If the power went out during a monsoon, too bad—you better have a generator. We did. No AC when the generator ran, but the lights and computers stayed on.

Internet was so unreliable we had three providers. Our teammate Prosper slept in a spare room at the office. The janitor, Majeed, would heat water in a bucket so he could shower. Really.

One night Prosper accidentally deleted the production database. That's how we learned backups matter. Another time, after working all night, he tried helping a girl reset her password. He ended up resetting *everyone's* password to "Sunday."

But the thing that made it work was the people. We found raw, underrated talent in Pakistan. Our first hire, Noman—Nomi—became our fourth co-founder and eventually ran Peanut Labs.

Rahil, one of our early senior engineers, was brilliant and loud, constantly arguing with Prosper but also filling our code comments with "Your Mom" jokes for Prosper.

It was chaotic. It was duct tape and adrenaline. But it worked. It felt like we were building a small part of the future. We were riding the wave.

• • •

DOING STARTUPS IS SOMETIMES LIKE SURFING, CATCHING A BIG WAVE. BEING AT THE RIGHT PLACE AT THE RIGHT TIME.

SOCIAL NETWORKING WAS THE BIG WAVE BACK IN 2005, LIKE MOBILE IN 2010, AND LIKE AI IS NOW.

• • •

MOVING TO SAN FRANCISCO

In Pakistan, we tried recruiting engineers the hard way: giving talks to graduating classes and inviting anyone ambitious to apply. The office was half underwater—literally. On Rahil's first day, it flooded, and water was streaming down the stairs while candidates came in for interviews.

That's when Prosper interviewed Nomi. Five minutes in,

Prosper realized interviews like this were kind of a waste. So he pointed to a feature someone else had been struggling with for weeks and said, "Build this. You've got 24 hours. You probably will fail." Prosper gave him an impossibly hard challenge. Nomi did it overnight. He got the job. Later he admitted he only did it out of spite—just to prove Prosper wrong. And to add "Your Mom" jokes in the codebase.

From then on, that was the interview process: give people real work. No resumes. No theory. Just give them something hard and see if they can do it.

The Xuqa offshore team in Karachi.

Building the team in Pakistan did have advantages. The best engineers didn't come from the top schools. The kids from the top universities had ego; they'd show up like they were doing *us* a favor. The hungry ones—technically solid, under-recognized, and still out to prove something—came from the lesser-known places. Same story we'd seen with Harvard and Stanford grads back in the US.

And we could hire a lot more of them. A junior developer earns about $800 to $1,200 a month. They spoke English, worked US hours, and equity wasn't even the biggest incentive. A visa was. A shot at moving to Silicon Valley changed everything for them.

When they moved to San Francisco, they had nothing. No friends, no housing, no clue what to eat. We put them up in our townhouse downtown. Eventually it turned into a hacker house: three bedrooms, 10 people, mattresses everywhere. Our neighbors were the same—other startups crammed into shared spaces. The first Y Combinator batch was a few doors down from us. We played beer pong with the founders of Dropbox, Twitch, and Cruise when those companies were barely more than ideas.

Murti: Xuqa's first year ended with us back in the US, raising another $1 million from VCs. The three of us—Ali, Prosper, and me—took turns flying back to Pakistan to keep things on track. If no one was physically in the office yelling, people wouldn't show up. It was getting hard to build a Silicon Valley startup with most of our team offshore. We eventually started moving our best people to San Francisco—Saad, Salman, Ali Kapadia, Nomi, Rahil, and others.

One of the best parts of doing startups is this: looking back and realizing how many lives you helped elevate in a different direction. Across our companies, we helped over 50 people immigrate—from Pakistan, India, Ukraine, China, Eastern Europe. Some of them went on to run engineering at major companies. A few became VPs. It's not the stuff you put in a deck, but it's real. Prosper now runs an engineering team at Google. Nomi is at Meta (Facebook). Rahil runs an engineering team at Shopify.

NON-MONETARY REASONS ARE OFTEN MORE IMPORTANT THAN BONUSES OR EQUITY IN MOTIVATING PEOPLE.

MEETING SEDA

Murti: At one point, we hired a part-time guy in Europe to help run part of the community. Users hated him. He was creepy, kept making weird comments, and eventually we found out he was wanted by Interpol. Seriously.

A moderator named Seda, based in Turkey, started leading a full-blown user rebellion against the creepy dude. At some point, she found my profile and sent me what was basically a "Can I speak to the manager?" message.

She wrote: "I heard you're the founder. Who is this guy, and can you please fire him?"

I looked at her profile and thought, *Oh, she's cute.*

She ended up coming to the US for a language program—and to meet me. We've been together ever since. Fifteen years and counting.

MEETING ZUCK

The world map in 2006 was split amongst different platforms that dominated different regions and geographies:

REGION	TOP SOCIAL NETWORK
Brazil, India, Pakistan	Orkut
Japan	Mixi
Korea	Cyworld
Latin America	Hi5
Netherlands, Scandinavia, Australia	Habbo Hotel
Philippines, Malaysia, Indonesia, Singapore	Friendster
Russia	VKontakte
Turkey	Yonja
Turkey (colleges), Iran, North Carolina (US)	Xuqa
UK	Bebo
US, Canada, Europe	Myspace
Dating and Games	Tagged
High Schools	myYearbook
Open to all, not friends	Twitter
Professional, Work-related	LinkedIn
Universities and Colleges	Facebook

Most of these networks had tens of millions of users. Some like Myspace had hundreds of millions. But Facebook was most directly competitive with Xuqa, exclusively focused on colleges and universities.

The question at Xuqa was simple: what could we do to grow that would bring lots of users and retain them?

Gmail had just launched with 1 GB of free storage, and people were begging for invites. So we did the same—offered 1 GB of photo storage to every user. Facebook, at the time, only let you upload a single profile photo. We had full albums and a usage bar on your profile. It worked. Users loved it. Growth picked up.

Then Facebook copied it. Just like they'd copied events from iVentster. Just like they'd copy our virtual gifting later—pixel for pixel. At one point, Zuckerberg was logging into Xuqa five times a day from his Harvard email address. Watching us.

That was kind of his thing. Twitter gave him the newsfeed. Snapchat gave him Stories. Whatever couldn't be copied, he later bought—Instagram for $1 billion, WhatsApp for $19 billion.

In early 2006, on a trip to San Francisco, we dropped by Facebook's office unannounced. YOLO, why not, right? They had maybe 12 employees, a couple million users, and a small second-floor office above a sushi place in downtown Palo Alto. There's a plaque there now—"Facebook's first office." At the entrance was a mural and piles of Linux penguin plushies from their server vendor (they bought a lot of servers). The place looked like what it was: a scrappy, fast-growing startup run by kids. They weren't so different from us yet.

We walked in, and they were surprised but let us in to meet. Mark Zuckerberg was there, Dustin Moscowitz, Sean Parker; it was like *The Social Network* movie come to life.

At that time, Myspace was much bigger—hundreds of millions of users. Friendster was bigger too. But Facebook was exclusive—Ivy-league colleges only, verified by your .edu college email address. They were building the highest-quality network that everyone else wanted to be a part of. Myspace was struggling with fake profiles, low-quality randos, and spam. Friendster was struggling with technical scaling issues.

Facebook had already copied our core features—photos, events, gifts—so we said, half-joking, half-serious: "Look, you're clearly winning. You're crushing everyone. Just tell us what you're planning to do, and we'll get out of the way. We'll pivot."

Zuck didn't flinch. "No," he said. "I'm not going to tell you anything. We'll fucking crush you, and then we'll continue to do whatever we want."

For real, he said that.

That's when we learned that Zuck was extremely focused and completely ruthless. He never took his eyes off the product and what users wanted; he was also ruthless to everyone, including his own. Long before *The Social Network* showed how he screwed over his early co-founders with equity dilution and got mired in lawsuits, we walked away from that meeting thinking, "Wow, this guy is super smart, but he's an *asshole*."

Never meet your heroes.

That was crushing. As we left the building dejected, Zuck, Sean, Dustin, and the Facebook team threw the stuffed Linux penguin plushies at us from the roof of their office building. In the middle of the afternoon. Right on the street in downtown Palo Alto.

It was wild.

Ali: At the time, I didn't take it too personally. I laughed, caught a penguin and took it home with me. I kept one thinking that if Facebook became huge one day, maybe this penguin would be worth a lot. But I lost it during one of my moves.

The Linux penguin plushy that Zuck & team threw at us on the streets of Palo Alto

Everyone says social networks are about scale. But Facebook beat networks far larger than itself: Myspace, Friendster, Orkut. What actually mattered was exclusivity and quality. They built the place everyone *wanted* to be. Not just more users—better users.

You could see the same thing years later during COVID-19. Clubhouse launched as an invite-only audio network. At first, it worked. The quality of conversation was high. Then they opened the gates. The quality dropped, and so did Clubhouse. Same with Quora. When it was closed and curated, the content was exceptional. Once it opened up, the value leaked away.

. . .

NETWORK PLATFORMS AREN'T JUST ABOUT SCALE. THEY'RE ALSO ABOUT STATUS. PEOPLE GO WHERE THE BEST PEOPLE ARE—NOT JUST WHERE THE MOST PEOPLE ARE.

. . .

CHAPTER 4

NUDES, PEANUTS, AND SURVEYS

For about 18 months, Xuqa was the biggest social network in Turkey. Mobile telecom networks were even offering free internet access to Xuqa on their networks. Students at some Turkish colleges made their own Xuqa ID cards and carried them on campus. We had no idea why we were popular there, so we flew to Istanbul, threw some parties, and tried to reverse-engineer our popularity so we could repeat our steps elsewhere.

We hit 10 million users. We were number one in Turkey, Iran, and the state of North Carolina for about a year. But everywhere else traction was stalling. Users were leaving. And eventually, Facebook's network effects steamrolled everyone. Mixi, Cyworld, Orkut—wiped out. Bebo, Hi5, Tagged, Friendster and Myspace—gone. Different countries, same story.

Myspace sold to NewsCorp for $580 million. Less than a year later, the value dropped to zero.

Bebo had been sold to AOL for $850 million. Then it too went to zero. Michael Birch bought it back a few years later for $1 million. That was the world we were in.

Metcalfe's Law states that when a network is 5X bigger than you, it's not 5X more valuable—it's 25X. Facebook's verified, high-quality users, and eventually their compounding scale, crushed everyone else.

By 2007, it was clear it was over.

Like many founders, for a while we thought it was a product race. It wasn't. It was a network race. And we were too far behind in the number AND quality of nodes. Like trying to ace a calculus exam by studying geography.

Facebook had exclusivity, quality, and fast college-by-college expansion. They eventually added high schools and opened up to all users. We had...Turkey. Eventually that walled garden, like all the others, fell too.

Murti: I started reading startup memoirs, the first being *Losing My Virginity* by Richard Branson. Then every founder story I could find. Not for tactics. For fuel. Because most days it felt like nothing was working. Any time I'd think, *Fuck, why are we doing this?! This is painful. Nothing is working.* Memoirs would fuel me.

. . .

WE WROTE THIS BOOK TO GIVE YOU FUEL.

**THE DOUBT NEVER REALLY LEAVES. EVERY
FAILURE TEMPTS YOU TO BELIEVE YOU'RE NOT
CUT OUT FOR THIS. THAT MAYBE YOU JUST
DON'T HAVE IT. READ OUR STORIES. READ
MEMOIRS. FUEL YOURSELF AND KEEP GOING.**

. . .

Eventually, our VCs gave us the classic line: you're smart, but you need "adult supervision." So they hired a CEO who previously ran business development at Cyworld. His answer to everything was "do more deals." But social networks aren't built on deals—they're built on users. He lasted a few months, burned most of our remaining cash, and nearly killed whatever was left of Xuqa.

Startups aren't saved by outside CEOs. They're saved by founders who have nowhere else to go.

We finally grew the spine to tell our investors: this is our company, and if you don't like how we're doing it, go fuck yourselves.

We tried to raise more money, but the VCs lost interest in social networking when it was clear Facebook was winning. So we tried to sell the company. We almost closed a deal with a Russian buyer—you already heard how that turned out. Murti drove overnight from Vegas to San Francisco. We laid off most of the team. Cut our salaries to zero. Had four weeks of cash left. We were scraping by to survive.

• • •

WHAT'S HOT WITH VCS CHANGES EVERY 18 MONTHS OR SO. WEB 2.0. SOCIAL NETWORKING. SOLOMO. CASUAL GAMING. MOBILE APPS. SAAS. FINTECH. MORE RECENTLY: VR AND AR. BLOCKCHAIN. DEEPTECH. NOW IT'S AI.

THERE'S ALWAYS A NEW WAVE. YOU SHOULD KNOW WHICH ONE YOU'RE IN—BUT DON'T BUILD JUST BECAUSE IT'S HOT.

• • •

FOLLOW THE NUDES

The nudes led us to our next pivot.

If you want to spot where technology's going, look at porn and video games. VHS, the internet, online payments—they all took off there first. The same thing is happening now with VR and AI.

Most consumer startups, whether they admit it or not, tap into one of the seven deadly sins: pride, greed, envy, lust, gluttony, wrath, or sloth. The best founders figure out which one they're serving and focus.

We had already added web-based games (poker, backgammon, okey) in Xuqa to boost retention—same playbook as Hi5. Ali Kapadia helped build what was at the time the world's best browser-based poker game. The games were free. They gave us engagement but not money.

Then we hit the wall with four weeks of cash left in the bank. That's when we realized we had to try charging users. Not later. Now.

Desperation is the mother of invention.

So on a Friday, we started limiting playtime and features in the games by adding a virtual currency called Peanuts (like a points system, levels, or XP in games). Users got mad. Something that was free was now pay-to-play.

We logged off over the weekend. On Monday, we discovered that users on the site had figured out who the CTO was and were messaging Prosper directly asking for more Peanuts.

"These girls, man," joked Prosper, "are sending *pics* for Peanuts, hehe."

"What do you mean *pics*?"

"Oh you know...like nudes."

OMFG.

It was happening with Rahil and other developers too, not just Prosper.

A light went off—if Peanuts were this valuable to some users, surely we could try charging for them? So we did. And immediately, that turned into a few hundred dollars per day in revenue!

Some users even paid thousands of dollars for peanuts. This was exciting! This could buy us a few more months of runway.

Girls on Xuqa sending holiday "cheers" to our engineers (this is the SFW version)

• • •

MOST CONSUMER STARTUPS TAP INTO ONE OF THE SEVEN DEADLY SINS: PRIDE, GREED, ENVY, LUST, GLUTTONY, WRATH, OR SLOTH.

• • •

PEANUT LABS

Charging for Peanuts started to work. But only about 2 percent of active users paid for Peanuts. Those that paid, paid a lot. But 98 percent didn't pay. Could we monetize that 98 percent segment in some other way? Ads?

Ali: I remembered seeing these annoying pop-up ads for surveys on the internet. They invited you to take a survey and win a gift card. Those surveys were free too. Could they be done without annoying pop-ups? Would the other 98 percent of our "free" users take a survey for Peanuts?

We went digging and discovered that there was a $50 billion market research industry, of which $7 billion was online. Advertisers in the Fortune 500 (think Procter & Gamble, Warner Bros, AT&T) typically commissioned market research for product development, for research, or to track ad spend effectiveness. Companies like Nielsen, comScore, TNS, and Ipsos would take on these projects, then subcontract out the online survey data collection to a bunch of vendors.

We took some of these surveys, put them on Xuqa, and users started taking them to earn Peanuts. We were able to monetize the free users who didn't want to pay money; they could pay with their time by taking a survey instead. We were earning on average $1 to $3 per completed 10- to 15-minute survey. Not a lot, but it could add up if a lot of people took them.

This felt awesome. We had finally figured out something users wanted to pay for, either directly with their money or indirectly with their time.

But Xuqa's user base was limited and declining. To grow revenues, we would need 10X more users, which wasn't happening. We had finally discovered how to monetize users, but now our users were leaving. Argh! Where were we going to find more users?

At the time in San Francisco several consumer services were gaining in popularity: LiveJournal (the blogging platform), Xanga (another blogging platform), and HotOrNot (the viral social app). They had tens of millions of users.

Could we tap into their audiences instead?

Xuqa, via nudes-for-Peanuts, thus became a B2B survey company. We called it Peanut Labs. Never forget where you come from.

But when has anything ever gone according to plan?

SORRY, YOU CAN'T TAKE THAT SURVEY

We did several high-profile partnership deals with LiveJournal, Xanga, HotOrNot, and OKCupid. All of these services restricted some features and put them behind a paywall. Users could either pay them directly with a credit card or take a survey with Peanut Labs to unlock features.

Our service was embedded within all these partners' sites. It felt so cool to be working with well-known technology companies. Something our friends and parents might finally recognize.

What we didn't realize at the time was that these surveys had tons of qualification requirements. They were typically restricted to US and Canadian users. The average brand would look for a very specific profile, such as a 24- to 36-year-old female mom from Florida with a college degree and two kids. Other surveys looked for IT professionals, gamers, or doctors. And they were all capped at a limited number of responses (such as 3,000 successful responses). Users didn't know in advance if they would qualify for a survey, and many of them (like 90 percent) would be disqualified after two to three questions, leading to a poor user experience and no monetization.

These surveys weren't plug-and-play and didn't work to

effectively monetize our partners' audiences. We churned through and lost all our early partners—LiveJournal, HotOr-Not, Xanga, and OKCupid.

Shit.

Maybe Peanut Labs wasn't going to work.

We had to solve this "square-peg, round hole" problem quickly—get more users into surveys without those surveys rejecting them. And we needed a cheaper, more abundant source of traffic that had less of an opportunity cost.

Nomi, Murti, and Prosper came up with this concept of a "survey router": saving a user's demographic profile by asking them to do a mini-survey from Peanut Labs in advance. They were guaranteed a small, near-instant reward, which made users very happy. We would only show them advertisers' surveys if there was a high likelihood of a match.

Our sales team led by Sean and Matt also struck a key deal with our largest customer, Ipsos, that gave us a consistent supply of $100,000 to $200,000 worth of survey inventory each month.

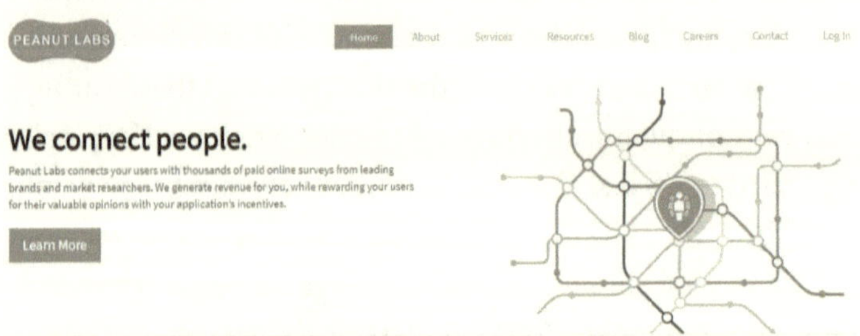

The old Peanut Labs website: "Peanut Labs: connecting researchers with audiences on social platforms and games"

This solved the product problem to a large extent—the first-time user experience was now 10X better with our survey router, instant rewards, and deep inventory of surveys.

. . .

USERS PREFER FREQUENT, SMALLER REWARDS TO LARGER, INCONSISTENT ONES. CONSISTENT REWARDS ARE BEHAVIOR-FORMING.

. . .

Would the new system work for our partners? We went back to ask.

No. They were done. They were making more revenue just charging users with credit cards. There were trade-offs for them in user retention and experience by adding more monetization levers. They weren't going to try again.

Fuckkkkkk.

. . .

YOU ARE LIKELY GOING TO BURN THROUGH YOUR FIRST FEW PARTNERS FOR PILOTS, SO IT'S BEST TO START WITH SMALLER PARTNERS FIRST AND STAGGER THEM.

. . .

We were running low on cash again too. But this time was worse—Xuqa was declining, a buyer had just walked away from buying Xuqa, and we had just lost all our partners for Peanut Labs.

Goddamn it.

WHAT FACEBOOK TAKETH AWAY…FACEBOOK GIVETH

Ultimately, Facebook killed Xuqa, just like it killed all the other social networks. We sold off Xuqa to our buddy Zaki and his team that included Raheel and many of Xuqa's key people. This bought us a few more months. Zaki and team eventually used Xuqa to launch several more games, and the community continued for a few more years.

At the same time, we weren't making progress on Peanut Labs. Things looked dire. Then in late 2007, Facebook launched something incredible—a new Facebook App platform for developers. Developers could now build mini-apps on Facebook, and launch them to hundreds of millions of users.

Wow. But why?

Facebook knew they couldn't build everything users wanted. No one could. So instead of trying, they opened their platform. Let third-party developers build the features.

It was a smart bet: developers got distribution, users got more things to do, and Facebook got a growing ecosystem that made it harder for anyone else to catch up. The platform became the moat.

Murti: I was following this new platform launch and some of the very first apps on it. I messaged the developer Mike Sego of this pet app called Fluff Friends. It was like Tamagotchi, a game where you adopted, fed, and cared for your very own virtual dog or cat. If you ran out of pet food, you had to invite your Facebook friends to get more.

The crazy part? This invite mechanism generated notifications to all of your friends. People check their notifications daily. Hundreds of your friends would click through, install the app (like a widget for your Facebook page), and start their own pets. Nobody wanted their pet to die.

We had never seen anything grow this fast.

Mike did what a lot of early developers did—he got millions of users fast, with no real plan to make money. He tried ads first, but the rates were terrible. Not enough to matter. So we walked him through what a virtual currency was (given our Peanuts experience) and how to use it in his app. His app already felt like a game, so it fit naturally. Once he had payments flowing, he layered in credit cards. Then surveys from Peanut Labs. There was no grand strategy, just a lot of trial and error. Throw spaghetti, see what sticks.

When users ran out of pet food, they could either invite their friends, pay $10 with a credit card, or take a free online survey. Users didn't want their pets to starve—they took surveys all day long.

This time, everything finally fucking worked.

Tens of thousands of users were showing up consistently each day to take surveys. We clocked our first $100K month in revenue.

And just in time. We were completely out of money. Maybe now with this new traction, somebody would want to invest? It wasn't a slam dunk from an investor's POV, but maybe just enough?

I pinged every fund I could find. Thousands. Took over 100 meetings. Spent six months driving up and down 280 from San Francisco to Sand Hill Road. That stretch of highway is seared into my brain forever.

And I hated every second of it—because all I ever heard was *no*. Imagine 100+ meetings with brilliant people, and every one of them tells you you're not good enough. What does that do to your optimism? Your self-worth?

Most days, I felt like throwing up.

Ali encouraged me to just keep going, not to take it personally, but how could I not? They weren't just rejecting the business; they were also rejecting us.

Then I met a tiny VC fund run by two people, and Pete from Leapfrog Ventures said yes. We ended up closing a $3.2 million funding round.

Thousands of investors emailed. Over 100 meetings. And one yes.

We just needed one. We would survive.

We have been called cockroaches by our investors and well-meaning friends. Roaches were reportedly found in Hiroshima and Nagasaki after the atomic blasts. They can take a serious beating and keep going. That pretty much describes the startup experience.

Another way to describe the startup J-curve is this: the part that looks flat is basically *getting punched in the face*, and the part that goes up is what you read about in Techcrunch.

All that advice about scaling, finding PMF, hiring, raising money—it's all irrelevant if you cannot take a fucking beating.

. . .

"IT AIN'T ABOUT HOW HARD YOU CAN HIT. IT'S ABOUT HOW HARD YOU CAN GET HIT AND KEEP MOVING FORWARD."

—ROCKY BALBOA

. . .

ROCKET SHIP AND BUILDING COMMUNITY

Facebook was very generous in the early days of 2008 and allowed app developers to send out millions of notifications *per day*. As a result, many of the early apps—Mafia Wars, Fluff

Friends, Vampires and Zombies, Causes—grew to millions of users within weeks.

One such app, Pillow Fight—run by our friends Anand and Shikha Chhatpar—got to 15 million *daily* active users within a few months.

Zombies and Vampires by Blake Commagere. Dope Wars by Roger Dickey. Best Friend Predictor by Ankur Nagpal. Farmville by Amitt Mahajan (Zynga). Mob Wars by Dave Maestri. I Heart by Atif Nazir. These sound like silly apps, but they had 100 million more users than most startups ever will.

The space was *exploding.*

Ali: I was in Mountain View for lunch with a friend, Kevin Chou. His startup called Watercooler was struggling, unable to raise money. At lunch he said they were out of options and had to pivot. They would go all-in and build a game on the new Facebook platform. It was this or bust. The game was called Kingdoms of Camelot, and they'd rebrand the company as Kabam.

Three years later Kabam was acquired by South Korea's Netmarble games for $800 million.

Zynga started as a humble developer of a poker game on Facebook. Their lead developer lived in our apartment and complained about the game. He said he didn't really believe in this poker game, but they were trying stuff, and they were paying him well. Four years later Zynga IPO-ed at a $7 billion market cap.

We worked with most of these people and companies like Electronic Arts, Nexon, Ubisoft, and well-known game developers.

When we started writing this book, we asked Prosper what he remembered about these days. Here's what he said:

> Ali's always been the quiet godfather. He's not the guy working the room or handing out business cards, but somehow he builds the best networks—usually by throwing the best parties.

> The people who showed up weren't random. They were the right ones. That's where the connections happened. That network helped build Peanut Labs—hiring, intros, fundraising. Everything starts with community. Need a beta tester? Covered. A partner? Done. An investor? Already there.

> And once the party got going, Murti brought the energy. He turned the gathering into momentum.

Murti got into a community of pickup artists around that time—he went to a bunch of events and even coached other guys in the art and science of talking to girls. And that became an inflection point and personal unlock for us because if you get in the terrifying habit of talking to girls who are complete strangers at bars and clubs, you end up having no fear whatsoever at talking to random prospects at conferences. Girls are far, far more terrifying.

One of the more memorable events was at the Game Developers Conference. We hosted a pirate-themed yacht party on the water each year. It was black tie, invite-only, and I set the ticket price to $2,500. People saw the high price and instinctively wanted in. We gave free tickets to all our VIP prospects, of course, who never turned down the invite. It became viral.

Year one: all free passes. Year two: a couple of people actually paid. Year three: people regularly buying tickets at retail, sold out. The *Wall Street Journal* even wrote about it.

Peanut Labs: building community through parties

• • •

FOUNDERS DEFAULT TO ISOLATION. THAT'S A MISTAKE. COMMUNITY ISN'T JUST GOOD FOR THE SOUL—IT'S GOOD FOR BUSINESS.

• • •

Twenty years later, we've remained friends with many of the people we met or worked with. Some of our closest friends have come from this time. They've become like family. We are raising kids, and our kids are now friends too. Nothing beats that. Nothing in life compounds as much as friendships over 20 years. It was the most special part of building Peanut Labs.

**TRAP ALL YOUR WARM LEADS ON A BOAT FOR
FOUR HOURS. NO SELLING. JUST FUN. THEY'LL
REMEMBER YOU WHEN THEY NEED YOU.**

LESSONS FROM PEANUT LABS

Ali: At some point, we had a lot of users but not enough surveys. Ali and Anya Shapina (our Developer BD team) were signing up too many game and app developers. It was always a balancing act. We had to scale up the research and advertising side to match. Brands to market researchers, we targeted anyone who needed data. Developers gave us access to users. Researchers gave us money to run surveys.

We hired our first Head of Survey Sales, Kristen. She had potential. Then a month later she just vanished. Not a word. Days later, we found out she'd attempted suicide. Murti and Prosper flew out to Texas to track her down and meet her. Just showing up made a difference. She was suffering from depression and was really touched that someone cared enough to check in on her. She got help. Today, she's a life coach and thriving.

Next came Sean, a market research veteran in Seattle. He didn't want to move, so we opened a Seattle office. It grew to 25 people. Sean built a real and effective sales and account management organization. But now we had two offices, two cultures. Seattle sold things San Francisco couldn't deliver. Sales said yes to everything. Product yelled no after the fact.

Here's how a typical week looked:

- Seattle Sales: "We sold 6,000 Linux sysadmins for $5 per survey. Big $300,000 deal, huge win. Go deliver it."
- San Francisco Product: "We have teens playing Farm games. Not Linux sysadmins. Not for $5."

Conflict. This happens in every sales-heavy startup. Sales brings in revenue and assumes they're the core. Product and technology lives with the mess. Much of this could've been avoided by having just one office, one culture.

Eventually we brought in an industry veteran as our new CEO. He'd run a big ad research firm. He had spent some time on our board and had 25 years in the industry. We figured having someone like that running Peanut Labs could 3X our survey sales. It didn't. He was used to managing 2,000 people. At a 50-person startup you need urgency, not structure. You need accountability, not niceties. He didn't have founder energy. And he was remote—didn't sit in either Seattle or San Francisco.

It somehow got so bad we had just three months of cash left. We had burned through $3.2 million. Sales weren't going up. Expenses were. Nobody was holding the team accountable. How the hell did we end up in this position again, nearly running out of money?

The board wouldn't fire the CEO. So I told them: either he goes or the founders go. They fired him that afternoon. It was hard for him. But keeping the startup alive came first.

. . .

PEOPLE DEFAULT TO OPERATING LIKE THEY DID AT THEIR MOST-RECENT PREVIOUS JOB. A BIG-COMPANY EXEC WON'T SUDDENLY BECOME A SCRAPPY FOUNDER OR STARTUP CEO.

. . .

Our VCs, while invaluable and supportive early on, weren't much help later. They showed up once a month for a board meeting, ate sandwiches and salads, cracked awkward jokes, and then left. They complained about the food. They complained about how we were kids. They complained about how boring the research industry was. Most board meetings were distractions. During one meeting, one of the investors spent an hour on the whiteboard trying to explain to the other VC how our business worked. He drew all these squiggly lines, flow-charts, and Venn diagrams. Meanwhile, we sat there thinking, *LOL, this is not how our business works.* After three years on the board, they still didn't understand the fundamental basics of our business.

We've generally found that the best investors are recent founders who've suffered a lot, are deeply empathetic (a.k.a. beautiful people), and generally stay out of the way unless asked.

• • •

MOST INVESTORS MARKET THEMSELVES AS VALUE-ADD IN VARIOUS WAYS. IN REALITY, MANY ARE VALUE-NEGATIVE.

AN INVESTOR WHO SIMPLY WIRES FAST AND DOES NOTHING IS BETTER THAN THE MAJORITY OF INVESTORS OUT THERE.

• • •

THE EXIT

Our surveys were in hundreds of apps and games, taken by millions of users each month. On the web, on Facebook, on mobile. We added video ads, trial offers, and international payments. Revenue hit $15 million.

Everything went up seemingly overnight—at least it felt that way after four years of suffering, pivoting, and wandering.

Peanut Labs worked because we hit an unsolved niche: getting young people to answer surveys. But the real money was in software, not services. We missed that shift. Companies like Qualtrics and SurveyMonkey were just starting. We had a survey product in development, but we were too late and too distracted.

. . .

REVENUE QUALITY MATTERS. CHASING SHORT-TERM SERVICE DOLLARS LOCKS YOU INTO LOW MARGINS AND LOW VALUATIONS.

. . .

When we tried to sell the company, everyone told us to hire a banker. Rookie mistake. We paid $1 million to a bank. They promised intros to Google, Yahoo!, whomever. Nothing happened. The real buyers were already in our space—our existing partners and customers.

Eventually, one of our survey customers, E-Rewards, made an offer: $30 million, half in earnout. We took it.

Ali: I still remember the day we announced this to our team—their mouths literally fell open. I expected this would be the happiest day of my life. But all I felt was relief. Relief that it was over. Relief that we hadn't died. Relief that we had made it to the finish line.

The Peanut Labs team after we announced the acquisition.

We took the offer because we were tired and broke. After signing the deal, the acquirer stopped integration. They had 500 full-time salespeople who had promised to send us more survey inventory. No sales were sent our way. They deprioritized us to death, making the earnout impossible to hit. Prosper was already working on other startup ideas. We walked a year later.

One of our investors asked, "Should we sue them for not doing their part for the earnout?" We considered it, because the acquiring company had signed a deal, but in the end, we declined. It would only complicate the deal, draw out the process, and make life hell for the team still working there.

The deal wasn't huge. The VCs owned most of the company, so most of the money went their way. From what we made, the first thing we did was buy a house for our mother, one she had always wanted. We had a troubled childhood, but she did raise us and set us up for success. This was the least we could do to give back.

We're proud of the company we built. It was real. The community was enduring. We felt proud that we didn't sell a lemon. Many startups are duds that die or go to zero post-acquisition. Peanut Labs as a business continued to work well under Nomi's leadership for a decade after we left.

• • •

NEVER TAKE HALF YOUR DEAL VALUE IN AN EARNOUT. IT'S A TRAP. MOST EARNOUTS DON'T HAPPEN.

ALSO, DON'T HIRE A BANKER WITH HIGH MINIMUM FEES RELATIVE TO THE SIZE OF YOUR DEAL.

• • •

Peanut Labs taught us a lot. But after spending a year post-acquisition and not managing to get anything meaningful done, we were itching. Itching to build again.

CHAPTER 5

HIGEAR, AIRBNB, AND THE UNBUNDLING OF CRAIGSLIST

They had warned us about bears, rattlesnakes, and mountain lions.

They had warned us not to look anywhere but straight ahead when running, so as not to fall off the narrow, winding cliffs.

The problem: it was getting dark, and we were lost on the trail. We couldn't see the dangers we had been warned about.

We had fallen far behind our group, some of whom had already finished and left. We were still miles away. Would we have to spend the night here alone, under the stars?

Ali: Building and selling a startup feels like climbing a mountain, and many founders want to literally *climb a mountain* afterward. Mt. Kilimanjaro and Machu Picchu are regular favorites. We chose the Grand Canyon.

A few months after selling Peanut Labs, Erin (our finance lead and favorite finance person ever) found a hiking group that was attempting to run the Grand Canyon from one rim to the other. That's around 24 miles and 10,000 feet of climbing in a single day. It's called the Rim 2 Rim, and most people hike this over several days, camping in between. This overachieving group was going to run it in a single day, attempting to break the world record time of around five hours. The location was breathtaking: mountains, hills, jagged cliffs, streams, and valleys all inside a giant canyon. Fucking awesome. Nomi, Murti, Shane, Heather, Erin, and I signed up.

This was the kind of challenge we were supposed to train for, marathon-style. Most of the 50 or so others in the group were professional athletes. But Ali had fractured a toe a few months before, erasing all of his training gains while it healed. And neither of us had trained much for going *down* so far at that speed.

The Rim 2 Rim starts early, at 6:00 a.m. Because it's a canyon, you start at the top, run down, then across, then climb back out. By the time we got to the bottom, our quads were already shot and cramping; and it was just the beginning.

Soon Murti and I were far behind everyone else in our group. We even got separated from Nomi and Erin, who had run ahead. As Murti and I navigated alone, we missed all the water refill stations and ran out of water. Our legs were killing us. I popped some painkillers. We had to keep on moving. We ran the easy parts and hiked the tougher terrain and climbs.

For long stretches we had only each other to rely on. Stepping through puddles of donkey piss on our way up (donkeys are often used as pack mules there), the climb back just seemed endless. We talked to cheer each other up—"I think it's just beyond this hill." But it wasn't. It was fake hope, just to keep going. Eventually the empty water bottles and hunger wore us down. We slowed. We stopped for more and more breaks. Progress became a crawl.

As darkness approached, that hike became a physical, mental, and spiritual test. If we didn't make it out by the time the buses left, we'd be spending the night in the canyon without food, water, or shelter.

I was close to breaking, physically and mentally. Would we ever make it out? I looked up at the stars, praying for something, anything. We kept climbing slowly, one foot in front of the other.

"Hey, you guys look like you could use some food." What? A hiker appeared ahead of us out of nowhere. "Here's some warm rice and beef stew we cooked."

We'd never seen this guy pass us, but he had apparently gone by, climbed out, gotten food, and climbed back down into the canyon to find us.

It was the best warm stew and rice we'd ever had.

He was our guardian angel that day. Thank you, stranger, whoever and wherever you are. We ran into others who helped us refill our water. Having had dinner, and with full water bottles, we found fresh legs. There was only an hour left before the bus would leave the Grand Canyon. There was no time to waste.

We climbed and climbed. We ran and sprinted. We fell, scraped our knees and legs, but just kept going.

Finally, we made it out of the canyon just in time, grinning from relief. As we hauled ourselves up the path and into the bus, everyone inside cheered our return. As one of them said, we'd made it, and most importantly, we were still smiling!

We finished in 13 hours, just 15 minutes shy of the 8:00 p.m. cut-off when the buses were due to leave. Not quite the five-hour record. Not a clean sprint, but a grueling grind that tested us deeply.

What a beautiful picture of what building Peanut Labs was like: no billion-dollar exit, just a grind through and through, where we got to the finish line and a small win just in time.

For the next four years, as we journeyed through 20-plus pivots in the search for our next startup, we looked back on this experience and drew from it. Through each new idea and each successive failure, all we knew how to do was keep going. And it helped to try and do it all with a smile.

HAVING CO-FOUNDERS

Ali: That Grand Canyon hike was one more experience that bonded Murti and I together as a team. We made it because we stayed together.

We always advise solo founders to find a co-founder if they possibly can. So many times in business, there is no one else who can understand what you're going through or help you make the decisions you need to make. Your spouse won't understand. Your best friend won't understand. Your team can't help you think through things at the most crucial moments. They'll worry about every crisis and fear for their jobs.

Sometimes a business-minded founder knows they need a technical founder, or a technical founder needs a people or sales counterpart. Y Combinator also prefers teams of two; as they put it, their favorite combination is a builder and a seller.

Of course, founder fights are the number one reason startups fail. But we think that risk is worth it. Nothing can substitute for the value of having someone to go through all the hardship with, to offer perspective on business decisions, and to eventually climb out of the canyon with.

If you want to survive long enough to get to PMF, the number one thing you can do is find a co-founder (or several). Don't do this alone.

• • •

—CHINESE PROVERB

• • •

BUILDING A RESILIENCE PRACTICE

The number two thing you can do is build a resilience practice.

Like a lot of founders, we're curious and adventurous people, and we made the most of living among the natural wonders of Northern California. By the time we were in our mid-twenties and on our second startup, hiking was one of the things we'd each found to explore outside of work.

Murti: About a year before hiking the Grand Canyon, I picked up trail running. At one point, I did a half-marathon trail run every week. At those distances, it's as much a mental game as a physical one, and I loved the challenge to Just. Keep. Going.

Once I was on a 30-kilometer run when a young woman and an elderly man running together passed me. I had to see what was going on, so I caught up to them. It turned out they were a father and daughter, and the older man was *blind*. It's one thing to run a road race as a blind person in their seventies. It's another thing to run up and down mountains, across streams, and over roots and rocks. Of course, once they made it to the finish line, the two of them got the loudest cheer of anyone; they made a great team, the daughter guiding her father with her voice and her arm.

Those two runners inspired me; if they could run a 30K on a

difficult trail, what could I do? Distance running and other athletic pursuits are incredible experiences for building the skills to survive a startup. People are fundamentally lazy. *I'm* fundamentally lazy. But overcoming physical challenges reminds us what we're capable of and trains us to push through discomfort.

I also spent a couple of years on a deep dive into psychedelics after learning about Elisabeth Kübler-Ross and her experiences with DMT (Dimethyltryptamine). I researched DMT, learned about various psychedelics, and went on my first psychedelic trip with an ayahuasca shaman in Napa Valley. I continued to do psychedelics in spiritual settings over the next couple of years. It was life-changing; everyone should try it.

Most importantly, psychedelics allowed me to experience unconditional love for the first time in my life. We talk about unconditional love, but we rarely experience it. Our partners don't love us unconditionally. Our kids grow up and leave home to pursue their own lives and careers. Our parents come the closest, but their love still isn't always unconditional. But this pure love does exist. That day, after the 5-MeO-DMT session, I felt it from my dog, Thor. I truly believe he is my spiritual guide and teacher in this life.

Thor: the spirit animal

Ali: Murti and I attended one overnight DMT session together. The next day, I drove us home along a hilly road with the mountain on one side and the cliff face on the other—a straight drop down. As we neared a bend in the road, Murti said, "Slow down."

"Why? There's no one coming."

"There's a tree blocking the road up ahead."

Sure enough, as we rounded the bend, there was a tree blocking the road. DMT opened Murti's mind and allowed this premonition. Me? On that trip, DMT left me puking all night. But it also cleaned out my head and left me feeling buoyant and clear for months.

In college, when I accidentally took that class on Sufism, I learned that the poet Rumi is often cited as the best-selling poet in America. I had never read his work before this, but I felt like I belonged in his words—like I was reading things I had already known for years. I started meditating regularly with a Sufi teacher. It was tough—learning to let go and sit quietly in meditation for 20–30 minutes.

My wife, Sarah, says that on the days I meditate, I am a completely different person. Calm, measured, like a mountain in a storm. The days where I don't, I'm moody, excitable, like sand in the wind. Nobody can quite expose you like your spouse can, both the good and the bad.

Every founder needs to build a resilience practice, whether it involves hiking, psychedelics, meditation, or something else. You owe this to yourselves and your startup. If you tap out prematurely, there won't be a startup left.

These are some common ways founders can build resilience:

- Regular exercise, particularly challenging and competitive races or competitions
- A tight community of other co-founder friends who are empathetic and supportive. Many form small ad-hoc groups, but some larger well-known examples are YPO, Tiger21, EO, and mastermind groups.
- A loving family at home
- Prayer, spiritual belief in a higher power

- A founder coach
- Purpose, knowing your why (not money)
- Daily meditation

Think of these as layers on a cake: the more the better. You should ideally have several of these to help build deep tolerance and an ability to take punches.

. . .

. . .

AIRBNB AND THE UNBUNDLING OF CRAIGSLIST

Murti: I met the guy who stole my car.

He was a middle-aged white guy with a belly. I actually shook his hand, gave him the keys, and watched him drive off in my BMW 5 series, expecting him to come back a few days later.

I never saw him again.

This was 2011. We were still riding high on confidence from selling Peanut Labs and completing the Grand Canyon. We were both lifelong fans of the British car show *Top Gear* by Jeremy Clarkson. Ali loved sports cars and often spent hours on the car websites configuring various models he would buy someday. His first car was a 20-year-old BMW Z3 he bought for $5,000, because that's as much sports car as he could afford back then.

He eventually bought a Z4, but it sat parked in the garage most of the time. In San Francisco you don't need to drive daily; you can just walk. Sports cars, especially, get used maybe once a week. They're also expensive to buy, with taxes, maintenance, and depreciation.

All our friends had the same issue—those who bought sports cars rarely used them. They sat idle over 98 percent of the time.

Wouldn't it be better to buy a car and share it with others when it wasn't being used? Or rent from other car enthusiasts?

In a quest to answer these questions, we launched a luxury peer-to-peer car-sharing service HiGear, named after *Top Gear*. (We *really* loved that show.) In those days, there were two companies doing peer-to-peer car sharing—GetAround and Relay Rides—and they both focused on everyday commuter cars. We decided it would be more fun to run the same model for fancy cars like BMWs, Porsches, Ferraris, and Lamborghinis. We wanted to build for ourselves.

We raised $1.3 million in seed money with many of the same investors who funded Peanut Labs. We were off to the races!

• • •

REPEAT FOUNDERS WHO HAVE AN EXIT UNDER THEIR BELT ARE ABLE TO FUNDRAISE 10X–100X FASTER.

• • •

HiGear would be a marketplace where people could rent and share their sports cars with each other. We would help car owners and renters connect. We would manage insurance, logistics, safety, payouts, and inventory. It was weird pitching this to insurance companies who didn't really get car-sharing at the time, but we managed to get Berkshire Hathaway to underwrite a $1 million insurance policy.

But how would we get car owners and cars listed? We couldn't just launch with Ali's sole BMW. We asked all our friends, and some of them listed their cars. Kevin Chou listed his Mercedes SL AMG. Jack listed his Porsche Boxster. We even bought a Tesla for car sharing—one of the very first Tesla Roadsters, the one actually used in the Bruce Willis movie *Looper*. Bruce Willis had driven it himself.

It was a start, but not enough. How were we going to attract more car owners at scale to really make this marketplace pop?

We tried a bunch of things that didn't work. Ads. Emails. Car groups.

The one that worked was Craigslist—the 30-year-old website was still going strong (and still is to this day).

Emotionally speaking, people have one big obstacle that prevents them from renting their car to strangers: they worry about the damage someone might do. But when someone lists their car for sale, they're done with it. Doesn't matter if it's a Ferrari or Honda: if someone is ready to sell, they're no longer emotionally attached, and they're less concerned about it getting scratched or dinged.

So we needed to find people who were ready to sell, and what better place than Craigslist? When Airbnb first got started, they would message people who had listed their apartments for rent on Craigslist and ask them to try out Airbnb instead. We decided to try the same hack for luxury cars. When someone listed a nice car for sale on Craigslist, we would message them and say, "Hey, do you want to rent your car instead?"

HUNDREDS OF STARTUPS HAVE STARTED FROM THIS STRATEGY—PICKING A CATEGORY ON CRAIGSLIST, AND THEN BUILDING A DEDICATED PLATFORM JUST TO SERVE THAT CATEGORY BETTER. THIS HAS BEEN CALLED THE *UNBUNDLING OF CRAIGSLIST*.

Through this Craigslist hack, we got 400 sports cars in the San Francisco area listed on HiGear—Porsches, BMWs, Mercedes, Ferraris, even a Rolls Royce. If this was a traditional car rental company, it would've cost us $25 million to buy these cars for the fleet. We had gotten them for free.

As a founder, you have to make these scrappy moves that polished managers at a big company would never make.

UBER

Murti: Uber started around the same time as an on-demand black-car limousine service. It was expensive, but the wow factor and convenience of hitting a button on your phone and watching a car come to you in real-time on a map was incredible. I used Uber for the first time in 2011 and thought, *Hey, this is awesome. Maybe HiGear should do this instead.*

I spoke to dozens of lawyers. Could we do this without a taxi license? Without permits from the city? Was there any way to do this legally? They all said, "No, this is illegal. You will *go to jail.* Don't do it." We unfortunately took their advice and shelved the idea. Travis Kalanick, the founder of Uber, did it anyway. Travis never went to jail. Uber now has a market cap of $200 billion.

Was it illegal? Yes, Uber broke city and municipality laws everywhere they went. But consumers loved it. Drivers loved making extra money. It was hard to prosecute something that millions of people loved. Crucially, the laws they broke were things that would result in fines, not jail time. Cost of doing business. They weren't selling drugs. Just disrupting taxis with technology. Travis knew which laws he could break.

• • •

IF YOU'RE DISRUPTING A REGULATED INDUSTRY, YOU HAVE TO KNOW WHICH LAWS YOU CAN BEND, WHICH YOU CAN BREAK, AND WHICH YOU CANNOT.

UBER FIGURED THAT OUT BETTER THAN ANYONE ELSE.

• • •

MODELS, BOTTLES, AND FAST CARS

HiGear: Models, building an aspirational brand

We had the supply-side sorted (car inventory). To grow demand, we ran Groupon discount offers. Groupon was big back then. This quickly brought in hundreds of renters. A lot of them wanted a special car for special occasions like weddings, graduations, or road trips to wine country.

To run operations frugally, we hired some interns (shout-out to Julia). Some absolutely crushed it. Hiring interns—both at Peanut Labs and HiGear—worked really well for keeping enthusiasm and energy high. Hire for attitude, train for skill.

HiGear wasn't going to be a transactional marketplace. It was a lifestyle brand and community. We borrowed our friends' cars, hired some hot models, and did photoshoots. Those postcards and pin-up calendars were a hit. Car and Coffee meetups are a big part of California culture. We went to car meetups with exotic cars on display.

We threw some crazy parties in San Francisco where models showed up in latex body paint, playing off the car culture of glamour, girls, parties, champagne, and celebrities. At one of our parties at Infusion Lounge, some of the cast members from the TV show *Jersey Shore* showed up. Parked outside we had supercars like Ferraris and McLarens—the whole scene was very much the LA-Miami vibe.

HiGear may be the only startup in San Francisco to have gotten away with having models in *nothing* but body paint. Ninety-five percent of the people at the parties were car guys. They lined up to take pictures with the models, with huge smiles on their faces. It was worth the risk of pissing off feminist groups in order to make our customers happy.

Within a few months of HiGear's launch, we were off to the races. We went from a business earning nothing to grossing a million dollars a year within a few months.

At one point in 2011 the founders of Airbnb reached out.

They wanted to chat about acquiring HiGear. We were huge fans of Airbnb (still are), and after meeting Nathan, Brian, and Joe, we were even more impressed. They were exploring the idea of adding car rentals to an Airbnb rental—it was a natural fit. When people travel and book an Airbnb, they almost always also rent a car from somewhere.

Airbnb didn't ultimately go through with the idea. It would be a distraction, and renting cars had more risk than renting apartments.

Despite this flattering interest, we realized early on we had a shitty business model. We were paying 80 percent of the rental value back to the car owner, and nearly 15 percent to the insurance companies. To retain owners of these Lamborghinis and BMWs, we needed to keep the payback amount that high, but it was too high for us to stay profitable long term. There were significant transaction costs that included insurance, refunds, service, and support. Insurance was making more money per transaction than us, and we were doing all the work. On average, we were getting $30 per $350 rental after all costs were paid. Sometimes we even lost money. This thing had poor unit economics, and it would be hard to fundamentally change them.

Some other car-sharing services from that time, such as Getaround, ended up raising over $700 million, but the key insight we had—this business had poor unit economics— dragged them down despite their giant funding and scale. They IPO-ed, and within a few years their stock went to $0.

The one exception in this space was Turo, recently valued at $1 billion. Turo wisely focused on airport rentals, rather than city rentals, with people who built rental fleets of 5 to 20 cars and operated them like a small business. This led to different unit economics, and Turo may end up becoming a viable, valuable company.

Murti: Back to the middle-aged white guy who stole my BMW.

Within hours on the very same day in October 2011, this guy had four friends rent out four other cars on our network, including a Porsche Cayenne, a Porsche Boxster, and a Mercedes SL65 AMG. This was organized crime, and we were the target. All five cars were stolen on the same day, collectively worth $500,000.

Shit.

After about a month, the police recovered all five cars and determined a gang of organized criminals based out of San Diego were responsible. They were stealing cars for crime getaways and to do drugs. Three of the cars were abandoned, and one was found at a body shop—it had been trashed. The trunk of my BMW was filled with empty antifreeze bottles, and someone had clearly smoked drugs inside.

Thankfully nobody had died or been killed. But this was bad. Insurance covered repairs or replaced the cars, but our community's confidence was shaken. Peer-to-peer rentals had serious risks, and this incident exposed them. It was hard to sleep well at night knowing that anything terrible could happen to any of the dozens of cars that were being rented out each week.

At some point after this incident we realized that it wasn't worth it taking on this added serious risk with the poor unit economics involved. It wasn't worth the $30 to $40 we were making per transaction to risk $80,000 cars being trashed, or worse.

The math just didn't add up. So we decided to sell the HiGear website and pivot to something new.

We found some guys who had recently left Hertz and wanted to try peer-to-peer car sharing. They paid us $250,000 up front for HiGear and agreed to pay another $250,000 in six months. Then they never paid the rest.

We hired a lawyer and sued, but shortly after, the buyers stopped paying their own lawyers. Then the buyers declared bankruptcy and left the country. Then they returned, came out of bankruptcy, hired a new lawyer, failed to pay the new lawyer, and then declared bankruptcy again. They did this several times, until we finally gave up on trying to get the rest of our money. It was a masterclass on how to weasel out of paying someone what you had contractually promised.

From here we entered the desert—our longest, most painful stretch to date.

• • •

IN THE SHORT-RUN HYPE, MARKETING AND FUNDING CAN CARRY A STARTUP. BUT IN THE LONG-RUN, THE UNIT ECONOMICS AND MATH MUST MAKE SENSE. LIKE BEN GRAHAM, WARREN BUFFET'S MENTOR, SAID, "IN THE SHORT RUN, THE MARKET IS A VOTING MACHINE, BUT IN THE LONG RUN, IT IS A WEIGHING MACHINE."

• • •

CHAPTER 6

4 YEARS, 20 PIVOTS

In 2024, Nvidia's CEO Jensen Huang spoke to a packed auditorium of students at Stanford. AI was super hot, and Nvidia supplied the chips that made it all work. The moderator asked Jensen if he had any advice for the graduating Stanford class.

He noted that because they come from a great school, most Stanford graduates have "very high expectations... People with very high expectations have very low resilience. Unfortunately [for you], resilience matters in success.

"I don't know how to teach it to you except...I wish upon you ample doses of pain and suffering."[2]

The crowd laughed. Then fell silent, as they realized Jensen was being serious.

Pain and suffering.

After we had sold Peanut Labs, we felt like those Stanford students. We had done it—built, scaled, and sold a venture-funded startup. We went into our second startup HiGear with high expectations.

HiGear blew up.

Little did we know that that was just the beginning of our lessons in pain and suffering over the next four years.

LINKEDIN

It was now April 2012. We had $750,000 in the bank (of the $1.3 million raised for HiGear). And a completely blank slate. We had let go of most of our team at this point and had gotten frustrated with the slow pace of going from idea to code to launch. So we learned to code ourselves, at least enough to build and launch prototypes. Murti found Bootstrap, the UX framework that made web development much faster. That felt so, so good—we could now build and iterate at 10X the speed, reducing hops from neurons to code. Learning to code is doable, and you can have a real, useful product within a few months. AI tools today such as Lovable, Replit, vo, Cursor, and PDD have only made coding easier.

• • •

**AS PAUL GRAHAM SAYS, IF YOU WANT TO
REALLY BUILD A STARTUP, LEARN TO CODE.**

• • •

LinkedIn had an open API back then, and we built a few products on top of it.

The first was **OfficeGreetings**—a professional e-card app for sending greetings to your LinkedIn contacts. You could send holiday or birthday cards with a couple of clicks and keep your network warm. It had a built-in viral loop: every time someone received a card, they could send one too. OfficeGreetings grew to $250,000 ARR, then flatlined. Most users came in around Christmas and vanished by January.

The next one worked better. **SurveyReport** let you get anonymous feedback from your LinkedIn network and turned it into a Myers-Briggs-style strengths report. We charged $99 a year, and people paid. At its peak, SurveyReport hit $1.2 million ARR. Murti built the front end himself and, as our resident viral hacker, tuned the onboarding flow until the K-factor was greater than 1.

· · ·

IN SOCIAL APPS, K-FACTOR MEASURES VIRALITY AND IS A FUNCTION OF HOW MANY FRIENDS EACH NEW USER INVITES AND THE CONVERSION RATE OF EACH INVITE.

· · ·

The backend for SurveyReport was built by Nabeel, our CTO at the time. He was from Pakistan, and we'd brought him to Silicon Valley on an H-1B visa. We were a three-person team working out of a hotel basement near our apartment.

After SurveyReport started to take off, Nabeel left for a couple of weeks to get married. While he was away, we noticed something odd—the K-factor was slipping. At the same time, invites from suspiciously similar survey apps started popping up in our LinkedIn inboxes.

What the hell was going on?

We dug into the new apps and found they weren't just *similar*—they were clones. Line by line. Same bugs, same code comments, even the same Terms of Service text.

When we confronted Nabeel, he confessed. "I was getting married and needed some extra cash," he said. "Sorry guys. I thought it'd be fine. What's the harm in a clone?"

Face palm.

Kind of wild how someone could think stealing IP, code, and launching copycat products, *while still being employed*, would be okay. We canceled his work visa and fired him.

Unfortunately, Nabeel wasn't an outlier.

Zaki—our friend who had bought Xuqa—was shutting the company down. He had 20 engineers between Karachi and Singapore and asked if we wanted to hire any of them.

Ali: I flew to Karachi and was in the room when Zaki broke the news to the team. It was brutal. The only silver lining was that I was there to hire. Everyone was dejected, but at least they had a shot at a new job. We ended up hiring four of the 20.

Within a year, three of the four had stolen from us—selling code, poaching clients, or launching clones. No integrity. No ethics. No sense of ownership. The only one who didn't was Salman.

Salman prayed regularly, had strong family values, and took pride in his work. He also adapted fast—learned to move at our speed, worked night shifts to sync with us in California, and became an incredible developer. Eventually, he became our CTO, and we brought him to San Francisco on a visa.

After that, we were done with remote hiring. But the damage was already done.

Because of all the spammy clone apps flooding notifications, LinkedIn decided to shut down its open API for all developers with no notice. SurveyReport died overnight.

We went from $1.2 million ARR back to zero.

. . .

IF YOU'RE A PRE-PRODUCT-MARKET-FIT STARTUP, DON'T HIRE REMOTE FOR CORE ROLES. THE FOUNDERS, AND THE FIRST FIVE KEY HIRES, *MUST* BE IN THE SAME ROOM TOGETHER. BONUS POINTS IF YOU ALSO LIVE TOGETHER IN A TINY APARTMENT.

. . .

DATING, PRODUCTIVITY APPS, AND SHINY-OBJECT SYNDROME

Ali: I was single then—not great in photos and terrible on dating apps. I was better in person. The whole experience sucked for me and for most of my guy friends. The apps rewarded a certain type of guy, and founder-nerds weren't it.

So we built our own. **FabDates** was a dating app that flipped the experience for guys like us. Apple rejected it, so we relaunched it on the web. The idea was simple: men would post their dream date—a hot-air balloon ride, horseback riding in wine country, a Michelin-star dinner—and women would apply to go on that date.

FabDates reversed the entire dynamic. Instead of sending endless messages into the void, guys could post a thoughtful experience and watch applications roll in. Like building a recruiting funnel for your love life.

Women loved it too. A few of our friends were getting half a dozen dates a week. The traction looked promising.

Then Facebook started banning our ads. No explanation. We later learned this was common for small dating startups—unless you were Match or eHarmony and spending millions a month, you were collateral damage of the algorithm. No human review.

Even worse, the unit economics didn't work. Our cost per acquisition was three times the lifetime value of a user. The math just didn't add up.

Plus, we had the same core problem—dating apps sucked for most guys. Men average a 1 percent response rate on dating apps; women average 20 percent. Men have to send out 20 times more messages to get a positive reply than women do. Dating is a numbers game until you find *the one*, so Salman and I built a new product called **NumbersGame**.

It was basically an ad-spend tool for your love life. You could build a custom dating profile and target exactly who you wanted to meet through the Facebook and Instagram ads API.

Say you liked "28-year-old women in San Francisco who love video games and *The Simpsons*." We'd show your ad only to them. They'd see it, click through to your profile, and decide whether to connect. You set your own ad budget depending on how fast you wanted to fill your dating pipeline. For $250, the average guy could get 7–10 matches a week with no effort. Serious value for money.

Our friends loved it. They signed up, put in their credit cards, and started spending. One even set a $1,000 daily budget. It was wild. We'd basically built a self-serve ad platform for loneliness.

Then Facebook banned our ad account. No warning, no explanation. We made a new one—it worked for a week, then banned again. This cat-and-mouse game went on for months.

Facebook's moderation AI didn't like the images that got more clicks and instead of flagging the ad, would simply ban the entire account. We could either run inefficient, poor-performing ads, or get our account banned. Facebook made it impossible for new advertisers to run in "sensitive" categories like dating, personal finance, investing, or personal health. We tried back channels through VCs and friends, but nothing worked.

In hindsight, maybe we should've kept on trying. But no one else had the precision targeting Facebook did. It was the only game in town—and they didn't want us playing.

At some point, we stopped caring about the problems we were solving. We started chasing opportunities—anything that looked like it might work. This approach made us fast but shallow. We iterated like crazy but without conviction.

Here's a sample of what that looked like:

- **Subscription boxes** like ShoeDazzle or Lovevery. We built landing pages, took payments, no product behind them. CPAs were $75–$100. Too expensive.
- **Acquisitions.** We looked at 30-plus companies with revenue, including WooCommerce. One founder wanted out. We passed. WordPress bought it later. It now powers 25 percent of e-commerce on the internet. Big miss. *Facepalm.*
- **Facebook birthday calendar app.** A million users, zero retention. The Facebook viral window (2007–2009) was over.
- **Hedge fund.** Wall Street funding looked predatory. Friends in finance told us to walk away. We did.
- **Jobs newsletter.** Made $10,000–20,000 a month but couldn't scale beyond that.
- **HirevsNot.** A "Hot or Not" for job candidates. Went nowhere.
- **Corporate MOOCs (Massive Open Online Courses).** Same idea Prosper later tried separately with his startup. Both failed. Selling to enterprises is a slow, painful death.
- **Themepot.** WordPress themes. Hit $10,000/month, flat-lined.
- **Bizchat.** Slack before Slack. All mobile. We quit when SMS invites didn't go viral.
- **Email Cherry.** A Gmail extension for tracking opens. 50,000 users. 0.3 percent conversion. No growth channel.

In hindsight, we chased too many shiny objects. There's an argument for working only on problems you care about. There's also an argument for riding the next wave early. But jumping between *industries*—not just products—was probably too much. We weren't following conviction anymore. We were chasing momentum.

• • •

**WHEN YOU JUMP BETWEEN ENTIRELY DIFFERENT
PROBLEM SPACES OR INDUSTRIES, YOU LOSE
ALL YOUR ACCUMULATED LEARNINGS IN THAT
SPACE. YOU START BLANK, FROM ZERO.**

• • •

GOOGLE, FTC, OH F*CK

After struggling to grow our own Email Cherry Chrome extension, we decided to build an ad network for extensions. Mobile ad networks were booming, but no one had built one for Chrome.

Our first product was called **Free Weekly Apps.** It let desktop users discover and install free Android apps directly onto their phones. To make that work, we built new tech that connected a user's Chrome browser to their Google Play account. Free Weekly Apps actually worked—and mobile game developers loved it. They were driven by performance marketing, and this could be a giant new marketing channel for them.

Within weeks, we had $15 million in ad purchase orders from our old Peanut Labs clients. For once, it felt like we'd found something that could scale very quickly.

Then came the *oh fuck* moment.

A few users complained that apps were "installing themselves." They weren't—users had opted in—but confusion spread. Google noticed. They didn't like that we matched a user's Google Play email between desktop and mobile. Overnight, they banned us, delisted our clients' apps, and killed the product.

Losing our own revenue was one thing. Getting our friends' apps banned because they'd worked with us was brutal. We shut everything down—uninstalled the product from all users and walked away from Chrome entirely.

A couple of years later, just as we'd moved on, we got a letter from the Federal Trade Commission. Google had reported us. The FTC claimed privacy violations and spyware. Totally unfounded—but terrifying. Dealing with regulators for the first time felt like walking through a minefield.

We were innocent but didn't have the money to fight. Cases like this can cost millions in legal fees. We found a local lawyer, pleaded our case, and somehow convinced them we'd acted in good faith. No fines, no penalties—just a promise to tighten up our privacy disclosures.

Even so, the ordeal dragged on for years—stress, lawyers, endless Zooms. When Sequoia and Andreessen Horowitz later did diligence on us, this came up every time. They both cleared it and invested anyway.

But it was scary as hell while it lasted.

INVESTOR UPDATES

Even when everything was falling apart, we never missed an investor update. Every month, without fail.

Now that we're investors ourselves, we realize how rare that is. Around 60 percent of founders never send updates at all—unless they're raising money. Especially when things are bad. But that's when it matters most.

Each update, each coffee, each call—it's a dot. Two dots make a line. Three make a curve. Over time, that curve becomes trust. Investors don't just need to see you when you're winning. They need to see your thought process when you're struggling.

Writing those updates also forces clarity. As Paul Graham said, *good writing is good thinking.* When you write about what's happening—and why—you step outside the chaos for a moment. You see patterns. You make sense of things.

Those updates became our monthly report card. Our self-evaluation. And sometimes, our therapy.

HOW TO KEEP GOING

Looking back, most of the businesses we started during that period can be summed up in a sentence or two. But each one took months of our lives. Blood, sweat, and tears. Mostly tears.

Sometimes we pivoted too fast. Sometimes we chased ideas we didn't care about. But at least we didn't make the fatal mistake—spending years on something that wasn't working and running out of money.

Over time, we learned that the ideas that tugged at our hearts were worth paying attention to. Startups run on founder energy. When you wake up excited to work on something you love or care about deeply, you're more likely to keep going.

• • •

**FOLLOW THE ENERGY. IF YOU, AS A FOUNDER,
RUN OUT OF ENERGY, IT'S OVER.**

• • •

That doesn't mean clinging to something that's not working. We've seen founders do that, and it almost never ends well. There are rare exceptions—people who grind on the same idea for a decade until the market catches up (Replit, Figma, Airtable). But 99 percent of the time, stubbornness kills. Flexibility wins.

Pivoting, though, is brutal. You throw away everything you've built, then try to summon the same energy again from zero. Sometimes you have to rebuild the team too. You go through weeks or months of confusion, trying one thing after another that doesn't work. It sucks.

What kept us going was fulfillment—and each other.

Fulfillment isn't fun. Most people would rather scroll Instagram all day. Fulfillment comes from the grind—the slow process of making something real.

And when even that's not enough, you do it for your team.

Startups aren't families. They're sports teams. Families keep you no matter what; teams don't. If you don't perform, you're benched. But when you do, when you play at a high level with people you trust, that's where the magic is. You practice, you compete, you bleed together. You keep going for each other when there's nothing else left.

Energy is contagious. Negativity spreads fast, but so does optimism.

For us, the bond at the center of it all was the co-founder relationship. Nothing else could have gotten us through those endless pivots. We had meditation, exercise, psychedelics, and friends. But without a co-founder, there's no one who truly *gets it.*

Most solo founders keep going out of ego—their identity depends on being seen. That's why so many billionaires still tweet all day. They don't need to, but they crave validation. Dale Carnegie once said, "If you tell me how you get your feeling of importance, I'll tell you what you are."[3]

Maybe that works for some. But for us, it was never about ego. It was about each other—and the work.

CHAPTER 7

VULCUN ESPORTS

It couldn't have been scripted better.

David vs. Goliath. Vegas. Thousands of screaming fans at the Cosmopolitan casino. An arena fit to be a digital coliseum. The warriors? Competitive gamers who were the best in the world.

It was the IPL5 Global Starcraft II eSports Finals. Korea vs. the Rest of the World (ROW).

South Korea used to dominate eSports (competitive video gaming), and still does. Only a few non-Korean players could even compete. Hence to try and even the playing field, the tournament organizers had invited the top-ranked players from around the globe to try and beat the Koreans.

Starcraft is played one vs one. Korea and the ROW team each had seven top-ranked players. The winning player from each team would continue competing until they lost. A loss eliminated the player. Whichever team won seven games first, and eliminated all enemy players, won.

The Korean team had titans like MMA, Creator, Leenock, and Bomber. The ROW team had smaller names like Scarlett, Naniwa, Huk, and Stephano.

It began horribly.

The home crowd booed loudly as the first Korean player eliminated the first ROW player. Then the second. Then the third, fourth, fifth, and even sixth. The Koreans were up 6–0. They hadn't dropped a single set.

So far, things were going as expected. The Korean machine was crushing everything in its path. The home team was down to its last and final player—Stephano.

Stephano was a fan favorite back in those days. He was French, sported a large curly, puffy hairstyle, and played Zerg. It was now down to Stephano vs. all of Korea.

Stephano won the first game. The crowd went wild.

Then he won the second. Then the third, fourth, fifth, and sixth. He beat six Korean players in a row!

The series was tied at 6–6. Down to the final game.

Ali: Fans next to me were screaming. Standing up on their chairs chanting in one voice, *Stephano, Stephano, Stephano.* They were waving American and other flags. The Rest of the World had found its hero—someone who had beaten not just one but six of the best Koreans. In a row. This had never, ever been done before.

The air was electric. The arena floor was shaking. You just had to be there.

This was eSports at its best.

Going into the last set, Stephano was tired and made some mistakes. He eventually lost to Team Korea. But it didn't matter—he took it down to the wire, the last set, kept us in the hunt. Made us proud. Made it epic. To everyone there, he was our hero.

• • •

PEOPLE DON'T REMEMBER WHAT YOU SAID. THEY REMEMBER HOW YOU MADE THEM FEEL.

• • •

TEAM VULCUN AT THE LCS

Ali: We loved this stuff. We had grown up as gamers. My first computer was a Commodore 64. Before floppy disks were invented, you had to put data tapes into the Commodore and rewind them to run programs and games. When MS-DOS came around, we got a x386 and started tinkering. Video games got us into technology and to the internet.

We watched and followed Starcraft before Twitch.tv existed, back when you had to pay $10 just to get an HD video stream from MLG.

We weren't at the event only to watch this match, however. League of Legends, another popular video game, had launched its own competitive pro-league called LCS (League Championship Series). In between the 20 or so pivots after HiGear, we had hired Team FEaR after they qualified for LCS, and we met them at this event. They would join LCS as Team Vulcun. Another one of our pivots: a pro eSports team. We thought it would be cool. And hella fun. And it was.

People dream of owning sports teams. For us, eSports was sports. We ended up putting together a pro team for $15,000, and joined the first season of LCS in 2013. We named the team Vulcun with a "u," because Vulcan was trademarked by too many people, including one of the founders of Microsoft. We improvised.

Our team started slow, being too timid and not taking risks, usually in the form of early ganks (helping teammates get kills). We finished the first half of the season at number five, with a 43 percent win rate. That sucked. Murti flew down to meet the team and over a team lunch told them, "Look, you're playing too scared. It's okay if it doesn't work, but take risks. Do the ganks early. Make the plays. If you don't take risks, we're guaranteed to lose, and I'll replace you."

Team meeting for Vulcun at the LCS

Boom. That worked. Our team, particularly Xmithie and Mancloud, stepped up. We started winning. It was incredible watching our team live on Twitch each weekend, cheering them on. That was the same year that Jack Etienne started Cloud9 (commonly called C9 by fans), the same year C9 and Vulcun took the LCS by storm, crushing well-known teams like TSM, CLG, Curse, and Dignitas. We finished the final half of the season at number two, with a 72 percent win rate, just behind C9. We were also the first eSports team in the US to have a full-time coach—Kenma, who was Zuna's brother.

**THERE ARE FEW HIGHS IN LIFE AS FUN AS OWNING
A SPORTS TEAM AND HELPING THEM WIN MORE.**

The top three teams represented North America at the World Championships that year: C9, Vulcun, and TSM. And like most years, all of us lost to the Koreans. But hey, we did beat the best teams in Europe along the way.

We met the Vulcun players after the World Championship games. They had become famous and now had groupie girlfriends who worshipped them and followed them everywhere. They were not as hungry as before, not motivated to practice 10 hours a day and put in the hard yards.

At the same time, the eSports team business didn't feel like a technology business. Coaching the players, putting together rosters, and selling sponsorships for viewership was a very different business than building a technology company. It was becoming a real distraction from building and launching experiments and pivots. So we sold the team at the end of the 2013 season to one of our sponsors, and they renamed it XDG for 2014.

We sold the team for $100,000.

A year later, a Top 3 team in the LCS was worth $10 million.

A year after that, they were worth $100 million.

A year after that, $300 million.

Facepalm.

NBA and NFL team owners from the Golden State Warriors, the 76ers, and Cavaliers were buying stakes in these teams. So were VCs. Some outright sales took place at these valuations.

XDG (Vulcun) ended up crashing and burning in 2014 and got relegated out of the league because the players lost their drive, but still. Had we kept the team, and somehow managed to stay a top team, *oh man.*

Ali: I regret listening to my head, instead of my heart. My head said: this is a distraction, this is not tech, this isn't in any of the playbooks, this won't scale. My heart said: this is amazing, this is sports, fans love this, we love this, this is the future. It's clear in hindsight which one was right.

• • •

WHEN DEALING WITH UNKNOWNS, YOUR HEART KNOWS THE WAY FORWARD BETTER THAN YOUR HEAD DOES.

• • •

DRAFTKINGS FOR ESPORTS

When those 20 pivots didn't work, we were totally spent. Everyone was burned out, and we had no energy left. After selling Vulcun, we decided to let the team go, cut down to three people (Murti, Ali, and our CTO Salman), and do what we should have done after selling Peanut Labs: take extended time off. No work, no startups, no ideas. Just focus on ourselves and try to bring some balance back into life. Firing people never gets easier. Layoffs suck. We considered calling it quits.

Murti went to Tahoe to ski. Ali planned to bike in Marin. Salman wanted to spend time with family.

That lasted three weeks.

Something about letting go, even for a short time, allowed our minds to wander. Wandering is underrated. It's like thinking in the shower. The best ideas come when you're really not looking.

Fantasy Sports is big in America. Every year, 62 million Americans and Canadians participate—they make hypothetical rosters of their favorite players and compete for points. DraftKings and FanDuel put real money behind it. You could now join a league with strangers, pay an entry ticket, and win or lose real money. Because it was skill-based, it was not considered gambling. Traction was real—DraftKings raised $700 million, and FanDuel $400 million.

Could this work for eSports too, we wondered?

It was also a lot easier to try and copy a model that was already working in one market (traditional sports) and apply it to a different market (eSports) than to invent something new. Too many founders, ourselves included, default to inventing something brand new each time. You don't have to.

· · ·

THE CHINA STRATEGY: COPY SOMETHING THAT'S WORKING IN ONE MARKET AND APPLY IT TO A DIFFERENT MARKET: A.K.A. THE ROCKET INTERNET STRATEGY.

· · ·

VULCUN 2.0

The next League of Legends season started in four weeks in January 2015. This eSports fantasy league would have to be ready before then. Could we even do it?

Murti: We decided to go for it. I had gone to Tahoe to ski and unwind. Instead I sat at a Starbucks each day from 4:00 a.m.

to 9:00 a.m. coding, skied a little, and coded again from 11:00 a.m. to 11:00 p.m. each day. I was exhausted, in Fuck-My-Life mode. I built the front end. Salman built a real-time backend using Node.js. We got it done.

Meanwhile, Ali lined up marketing partnerships with all the leading League streamers on Twitch at the time—Imaqtpie, Voyboy, and others. Influencer marketing wasn't mainstream yet, so it was still relatively affordable. We would need maximum exposure at the start of the three-month season. Starting midway wouldn't work. So we committed to spend all of our remaining $150,000—which was supposed to last us six months—in a concentrated burst of marketing in two weeks.

Do or die in two weeks. This was it.

After four years and 20 pivots since HiGear, we were finally, completely all-in.

Down to three founders after HiGear: Ali, Murti and Salman with significant others

ZERO TO $12 MILLION

With all the marketing we were doing, Vulcun 2.0 took off. Millions of fans discovered us through their favorite streamer and found competing in Fantasy eSports incredibly fun. In four weeks, we went from nothing to nearly $1 million a month in transactions. Unbelievable.

We were out of cash, however. We had spent it all.

So we went back to fundraising. We thought we'd just raise a few hundred thousand, anything just to get us through the next six months.

Ali: Fundraising was hard; no one wanted to invest. Tons of rejections, even though we were repeat founders. At one point, we sat in a parking lot and had one of the only fights we've ever had. Murti was totally done. "Fuck you, this isn't working," he said. Fundraising can do that to the best of us. I convinced him to just help raise a few hundred thousand, walk into one more meeting.

That one meeting was with Naval Ravikant, the founder of Angellist.

There's strong power in many weak connections. I had met Naval years earlier and loosely stayed in touch. Naval watched eSports, and his girlfriend at the time was a Twitch streamer. He didn't care about all the details, but he knew he liked eSports and he liked us. He liked that through all the pivots, we had carried our investors forward. Apparently most founders don't do that—when an idea doesn't work, they shut the company down and start over. Investors lose.

After 15minutes, he said, "I'm in." Even more importantly, Naval decided to put together an investor group for us and raise $500,000 through the Angellist platform.

We walked out of that meeting thinking, "This is great, but it's not enough." FanDuel and DraftKings had raised *hundreds* of millions of dollars each in order to market and scale their products. We'd made a single company in Silicon Valley last on $1.3 million for four years, but this new idea was going to require a lot more money to do well.

What we didn't realize is how many important VCs follow Naval. Once he syndicated the deal, everyone else wanted in. We hate to say it, but investors are a little bit like sheep–always looking to follow the leader. When one well-known and deeply respected angel investor like Naval decides to put up a check, everyone else wants to do the same.

So we left our meeting with Naval at 9:00 a.m. and drove to our next meeting an hour later with Sequoia. We'd pitched Sequoia Capital and been rejected by them three times in the past 10 years. Sequoia has this mythical aura as the oldest and most-venerated VC firm, and we wanted to know what it was like to be part of that inner circle. We weren't optimistic.

Unbeknownst to us, in the one hour it took to drive from San Francisco to Palo Alto, the news about Naval investing had gotten out all over Silicon Valley.

We walked into Sequoia expecting to meet one partner: Omar Hamoui. Instead, we discovered 15 partners in a boardroom waiting for us. Legendary names were sitting there: Mike Moritz, Doug Leone, Roelof Botha, Alfred Lin. Holy cow.

Ali: I had actually pitched Roelof for Vulcun a few weeks earlier and been turned down, but since founders invest with a partner, not with a firm, we were free to also pitch Omar. On our first phone call, Omar had said, "This is weird. I like weird things."

So there we were in a full partner meeting at Sequoia.

Sequoia typically requires unanimous approval from all their partners to invest—at least no objections. One partner in the room liked us, but another had just rejected us a few weeks ago. How would this go?

When we raised money for HiGear, we'd learned to make the pitch emotional. These investors see 50 pitches a week, so we kept our slide deck and numbers to a minimum and focused on the videos of eSports stadiums filling up, of kids screaming for their teams, of hundreds of millions watching. Murti and I wore the shirts of the League of Legends team we'd owned before. People invest more with emotion than they care to admit. They have to feel you before they believe you.

In our meeting with Naval earlier that morning, he'd said, "Look. If they like your pitch and decide to invest, they're going to try and make you sign a term sheet right there in the office before you head out. Don't do it."

That's exactly what happened. Sequoia sent us to a waiting room. Then they made their decision, went to a printer, printed out a term sheet, and said, "Here. Sign now."

The deal was a $4 million investment at a $12 million valuation. Holy shit, what?! An hour ago we had no money.

But based on Naval's advice, we walked out. "Thank you very much," we said. "We need to sleep on it."

We walked out on freakin' Sequoia Capital.

Right after that, we had a meeting at another VC firm, Matrix. Again, all of the partners were in the room when we arrived; word had somehow already gotten out that Sequoia had given us a term sheet. The Matrix partners were excited before we walked into the room and even more so when we said, "We can't really say what firm we met with, but they did offer us a term sheet, and we have a couple of days to decide." Eighty percent of the time, it doesn't matter who you are or what you're doing—if you have a term sheet already, the next VC will also say, "Yes, sign me up." That's follow-the-leader, herd dynamics at work.

Before we left that meeting, Matrix offered us a $30 million valuation, as if to say, "Take our money instead, please."

That was a Thursday. The next Tuesday, we had dinner in San Francisco with Omar from Sequoia, went back to our office at 10:30 p.m., printed a term sheet from our office printer, and signed the deal for $12 million cash at a $40 million valuation.

This is the story of our "overnight success." In the course of a few days, we went from running out of cash and fighting in the parking lot, to a $12 million valuation, to $30 million, and then to a $40 million valuation.

So many founders think, "If I can only raise money, I can hire people to build this thing and I'll be successful." But the truth is, we had to build the thing first, and it had to have traction first. Not just a straight line but a logarithmic curve upward. *Then* the moment we'd built something that was scaling exponentially, even the mighty Sequoia was at our door at 10 p.m. saying, "Here, please, sign my paper!"

• • •

CHASE INVESTORS, YOU'LL GET NOWHERE. CHASE CUSTOMERS, AND INVESTORS WILL CHASE YOU.

• • •

The startup world is so binary. We went from "nothing is working and the FTC is after us and we're wandering in the desert" to essentially God himself coming to our office to say, "Here, my sons, is $12 million cash from the best VC in town."

Part of that turnaround was the competition between investors. People who are fundraising often ask, "How should I value my company? What is it worth? What valuation should I fundraise at?" That's the wrong question to ask. We didn't walk into investor meetings with a valuation; we said, "We would like to raise X." X is a function of demand. Initially, it was a few hundred thousand dollars. After Naval put in a check, it was a couple million; after Sequoia, 12 million. The VC usually says they want 20–25 percent of the company to lead the round, so that's how the valuation gets set. It's a by-product.

DOING RIGHT BY INVESTORS

At this point, we were still the same legal entity as HiGear, rolling over the same shareholders. No one had lost money, which is important to us. Taking care of investors like this—making sure they get paid for their contribution—seems like a dying art, especially since the last boom era after COVID-19. When money is cheap, the old-school values of being honest, responsible, and thinking long-term go by the wayside. We've seen founders do selfish, stupid things because their mindset was "Let's fucking party!" or "Me first."

As investors, it takes a couple of years or so to know which founders are responsible and which ones are careless and rash. We've seen people steal; we know four or five founders who are on the run for straight-up securities fraud. But there are plenty of founders who are persevering, doing great, and treating their investors right.

There's no way to evaluate someone's character in a moment. We can look back at the 100 or so startup investments we made along the way and see that the late-stage companies were the worst bets. Companies with $10 million or even $100 million in revenue looked like stable, secure, blue chip investments but then turned out to be the most rotten, stinky piles of garbage, because people were either just exaggerating, or those companies couldn't keep growing fast enough to justify their lofty valuations.

In contrast, the earlier-stage startups were a bet on people. They'd change their idea five times, like we did, before they settled on the right one, but we believed in the founders and stuck with them through it all.

• • •

PEOPLE BEFORE PRODUCTS OR PROFITS. THOSE HAVE BEEN SOME OF OUR BEST INVESTMENTS.

• • •

The idea that there's comfort in predictability or scale hasn't borne out in our experience. Some of the "safest" decisions can turn out to be the riskiest ones. And risky stuff can work out to be the best bets. There's no formula to describe it; we've simply seen it happen across 100 different startups we've both invested in.

Elisabeth Kübler-Ross once said, "The most beautiful people we have known are those who have known defeat, known suffering, known struggle, known loss, and have found their way out of the depths. These persons have an appreciation, a sensitivity, and an understanding of life that fills them with compassion, gentleness, and a deep loving concern. Beautiful people do not just happen."[4]

VCs who've been founders themselves are the best investors, because they've suffered. When we meet other founders who are in that building, wandering-through-the-desert phase, there's a level of empathy you can't get anywhere else.

Over our years of suffering and struggling and trying to come alongside others living through the same thing, we've learned that we aren't just looking for investible businesses. We want to invest in beautiful people.

TO THE MOON

At this point we had raised $12 million, and Sequoia had put in another $4 million. The team grew to 70. Some of the interns we had hired previously—Marilyn, Aaron, and others—were now running teams of people. Murti ran product. Salman ran engineering. Ed ran business development. Chelsea did finance. We crossed $2 million a month.

Ali: I had gotten married a couple of years earlier. My wife, Sarah, saw only failure after failure, pivot after pivot. She supported me through it all. At an office party a few weeks after the funding round, she walked into our office full of employees, streamers, and users and remarked, "These ups and downs are wild." Later, speaking with her father who owned a successful business, she tried to explain "This is not like a regular business, or your business, Dad. This is something else completely."

• • •

"STARTUPS ARE LIKE THE OLYMPICS OF BUSINESS."

—SHAAN PURI

• • •

Some of our top users on Vulcun made $100,000 each. We called them "sharks." They were sharp, smart, and used data, not emotions, to make decisions. They often beat weaker players consistently and racked up six-figures a year. Noah, one of our top users, teamed up with one of our investors, Clinton, and started the eSports organization Immortals, which competed in LCS and other eSports leagues for several years.

We got the opportunity to attend Sequoia Basecamp—an

annual camp in the woods for current Sequoia founders. It was a peek behind the curtain at the inner circles of Silicon Valley. Elon Musk flew in on a helicopter. Jamie Dimon talked about the 40,000 engineers at JPM Chase. Charles Koch was interviewed by Patrick Collison. Satya Nadella of Microsoft shared stories of personal loss and making big bets. In breakout sessions, we were discussing struggles with the founders of Dropbox, Zoom, Trulia, and other publicly listed companies. These were the big effing leagues.

. . .

WHEN YOUR STARTUP BUSINESS CROSSES ABOUT $10 MILLION IN REVENUE, YOU CAN GET AN INVITE TO ALMOST ANY DINNER IN TOWN.

. . .

Murti: A week earlier, after skiing all day in Tahoe, I was sitting in a hot tub with my friend Kevin. He looked depressed.

"Kevin," I said, "What's wrong?"

"I'm selling Kabam [his startup] for just $850 million. It's only like four times revenue. I think we should be getting a lot more, but we're not."

"That's stupid. $850 million is an insane amount of money," I said.

"Yeah, but my friend Drew Houston [of Dropbox, had just IPO-ed] is getting 20 times revenue. Why aren't we getting that?"

A week after this conversation, I found myself in a breakout session with Drew Houston at Sequoia basecamp. He too was depressed after taking Dropbox public. I asked him the same question.

"Drew, what's wrong?"

"My management team sucks. It took a year to hire them. Half are useless. I have to fire most of them. And why is Zuck's team so much bigger than mine? Why is Facebook trading at 40 times revenue? We suck. What am I doing wrong?"

His buddy Zuck had IPO-ed a few years ago and was worth tens of billions.

That's when I realized: if money and "winning" were all I had, I'd never be happy. The rat race doesn't stop. The hedonic treadmill doesn't stop. It's ladders on ladders, all the fucking way up.

It was around that time that I committed to giving away everything I make over $10 million (adjusted for inflation). I figured if I couldn't be happy with $10 million, I couldn't be happy with anything. Ali joined in, and this has since become our own version of the "Founders' Pledge."

• • •

**"WHAT YOU KEEP, YOU LOSE. WHAT YOU
GIVE UP, IS YOURS FOREVER."**

—RUMI

• • •

Ali: Early in 2015 Jason Robins from DraftKings approached us with acquisition interest. I liked Jason. He started each day at 5:00 a.m. He was intense, soft-spoken, and kind. The deal was discussed around $150 million, but in DraftKings stock, not cash.

FanDuel, their competitor, acquired our eSports competitor AlphaDraft. It felt like the industry was consolidating.

Sequoia urged us not to do the deal. Omar said we should hold out for bigger. They brought in the heavy-hitters: Mike Moritz came to our office. "Don't sell, don't sell, don't sell!" We did not have access to core DraftKings metrics. They had recently raised money at what seemed like inflated valuations. There were some unknowns.

Mike Moritz from Sequoia at our office, urging us to turn down DraftKings.

I knew in the back of my head that at times like these, VC incentives are not aligned with founders. We are one of hundreds of bets in their portfolio—they need their good bets to grow huge. That's how they return the fund. They're willing to let many die in the process. For founders, all of our net worth, and indeed our lives, are in one bet: the startup we're building. For us a smaller, more likely return is better than a bigger, less likely return.

MOST FOUNDERS WOULD PERSONALLY DO BETTER ACCEPTING SMALLER ACQUISITIONS EARLIER IN THE STARTUP'S LIFECYCLE. VCS DON'T WANT THAT.

But it was hard to say no to legends like Mike Moritz. We'd had his quotes on our office wall before we ever met him. And here he was in our office, telling us not to do this deal.

We passed.

Today DraftKings is worth $24 billion. They've weathered ups and downs, reinvented themselves more than once, and my instincts about Jason proved right—he's a winner who's steered DraftKings to success against all odds. Had we sold, that $150 million stake would've been worth over $500 million today.

"IT'S NOT LEGAL"

Holiday party with the Vulcun team. Before things went south.

Cracks started to show. The sharks were winning too much. Casual players hated losing, especially when it meant real money. Lose twice and odds were you'd never come back. The system depended on sharks for liquidity, but they were also driving everyone else away. Tilt the rules toward casuals, and the whales with six-figure balances would leave. Leave it as is, and new players would keep churning out.

And then shit hit the fan.

A few weeks after we passed on the deal with DraftKings, everything blew up.

Both DraftKings and FanDuel had flooded the internet and TV with ads—hundreds of millions of dollars' worth. People got sick of it. And the questions started: *This looks like gambling. Why is this legal without a license?*

Then the *New York Times* broke a story: some DraftKings and FanDuel employees were using insider data to win on each other's platforms. In 30 days, daily fantasy went from legal in most states to illegal in most states.

Banks froze accounts. Visa, Mastercard, PayPal cut them off. And by extension, us too. The whole industry collapsed almost overnight.

In about 60 days, we went from making $2 million a month to zero.

It wasn't even our scandal. But we were too small to survive the fallout. To keep going, we'd need licenses in dozens of states. Betting licenses. Money transmitter licenses. Audits. Compliance. Geo-fencing users by legal jurisdiction. We weren't built for that. It wasn't just hard—it was impossible at our niche scale.

So we were left with two options: wait it out for years in court—or pivot.

We couldn't believe that after all we had been through, after millions in revenue, after going all-in and raising from Sequoia, after passing on a $150 million acquisition, it had come to this.

Back to fucking nothing.

This time was different. Much, much harder. We weren't three kids in a basement with nothing to lose. We'd raised a total of $16 million. We had 70 employees. Expectations were enormous.

Can you even pivot at that scale?

Just months earlier, we'd signed a seven-year office lease for our larger team. Spent almost a year on renovations. Hired an interior designer. Built an entry wall streaming nine live Twitch channels. The space could hold 150 people. We were scheduled to move in.

And then we had to do layoffs.

The timing was absolutely terrible, but there was no way around it. This was going to be the worst, most brutal layoff we'd ever done.

On day one in the shiny new space, we called 55 of our 70 employees into the biggest conference room. Everyone came in smiling, expecting big news. A fancy new office. A new product. A big partnership.

Instead, we handed out pink slips. The room went silent. You could hear the breathing. Some people cried.

It wasn't our first round of layoffs. And it wouldn't be our last. But it was the hardest.

We were left with 15 people lost inside a cavernous office built for 150. A giant space. A mountain of capital. And the unbearable weight of expectations we no longer believed we could meet.

→ *CHAPTER 8* ←

STREAMLABS

We eventually got out of that office lease we couldn't afford and moved to a much smaller, older office nearby. From a shining glass tower to broken plumbing and crickety floors in San Francisco. Like our very first office for Xuqa, the elevator here felt like it too would fall someday.

Vulcun had been shut down. We still had $12 million left in the bank, but no business. And we knew how painful and unpredictable it was to start something new. Thinking from first principles, could we use this capital to buy a business instead? Buy, then build? Just skip the *searching for PMF* phase?

Ed, one of the remaining team members, helped us scout deals. We looked at products we knew were successful within gaming, eSports, or live video. We didn't know business brokers existed, so we didn't use them. Turns out sticking to an area we knew was a good thing.

• • •

**GOOD BUSINESSES OR PRODUCTS ARE USUALLY NOT
LISTED FOR SALE. YOU HAVE TO GO FIND THEM.**

• • •

BUY, THEN BUILD

Acquisitions were not what VC-backed startups did with VC money. But Omar Hamoui, our partner from Sequoia, was a risk-taker. He liked things that seemed weird but made sense from first principles. As the founder of AdMob, he had built and sold the first mobile ad network to Google for $800 million. "You raised the cash to do something. So go do something with it," he encouraged.

Most other VCs would've said no or asked us to return capital. It's impossible to pivot a post-Series A company without a supportive VC partner. These tend to be former founders like Omar, who've been in the trenches themselves.

• • •

THE BEST VCS TEND TO BE FORMER, RECENT FOUNDERS.

• • •

We looked at dozens of companies and ended up closing two deals that couldn't be more different: CSGOJackpot and TwitchAlerts.

CSGOJackpot was a virtual item betting site, doing $10 million in revenue and $200 million in transaction volume. We bought it for $5 million in cash.

TwitchAlerts was a tipping and alerts service for Twitch streamers, doing $200,000 in revenue and $20 million in transaction volume. We bought it for $5 million, mostly in our stock.

We were all-in again on these two acquisitions. At least one of them would have to work.

CSGOJackpot was based on the popular first-person shooter game Counterstrike GO (CSGO), which had a vibrant in-game economy of virtual items called skins. These were purely cosmetic in-game items—you could make your weapons look cooler and thus stand out from other players. They were technically worthless digital items with no market value, but since players could trade them between themselves, they found ways to buy and sell these from each other peer-to-peer. Some of the skins were so rare they changed hands for thousands of dollars. On CSGOJackpot players could put their skins in a jackpot game where each player's chances were proportional to the value of skins they'd put in. Every minute someone won a new jackpot. The site did $20 million a month in transaction volume and $800,000 a month in revenue. It was throwing off cash.

It was the numbers that hooked us. After seeing many of our pivots with millions in revenue go up in flames, the prospect of a *post-PMF* product making serious revenue was enticing. Was it too good to be true? The founders were fighting and wanted to go separate ways. So they sold for cheap. Or so we thought.

Ali: Before buying this we had a legal firm do analysis on whether this was legal. It wasn't zero risk, they said, but very unlikely to be considered gambling since these digital items had no market value on paper. As the months went by, however, I couldn't help but feel in my gut that this opinion was wrong. These items *were* being sold for real money, millions of dollars. We hired an in-house general counsel, Al, and one day she came up to me and said, "My law school professor said 'One day, Al, you'll have a client that's doing something that's breaking the law. And you'll have to tell them so.'" She resigned.

It wasn't worth the risk, however small. And we certainly couldn't build a large, venture-funded company this way. We voluntarily shut down CSGOJackpot, even though it was doing millions in revenue and we had just paid $5 million in cash for it.

This was the fastest we had ever burned money. $5 million in 10 months. *Poof*, and it was gone.

• • •

DEALS WHERE YOU'RE PRIMARILY EXCITED BY THE NUMBERS, AND NOT THE TEAM OR PRODUCT, TEND TO BE *THE WORST*. CSGOJACKPOT WAS A STARK EXAMPLE, BUT WE'VE SEEN THIS REPEATEDLY IN OUR ANGEL INVESTING PORTFOLIO TOO.

• • •

CRAFTSMANSHIP, NOT BUSINESS

If this startup was a video game, we were down to our very last life. All the coins had been spent at the arcade buying more lives. Our pockets were empty.

TwitchAlerts was the exact opposite of CSGOJackpot. It had very little revenue—$200,000—not enough to justify a $5 million purchase price. They charged a 1 to 2 percent fee on tips to live streamers (people streaming games on Twitch). Private equity guys wouldn't even open a PDF to look at this deal. But we liked it because it had something rare—an organic growth flywheel. Each time someone tipped, say, $5 to a streamer, a live alert, run by TwitchAlerts, would pop-up on the Twitch video thanking them. Everyone watching would be encouraged to tip more. Some of the people watching were also streamers, and they'd say "I want that on my channel too."

We called this *monkey see, monkey do*. If something was useful, streamers copied what other streamers did. TwitchAlerts had started with one small Twitch streamer and grew organically to hundreds of thousands of channels from there.

The founder, Tom Maneri, was a craftsman. He cared deeply about what he was building. He was exercising craft, not building a business. He didn't care if this never became a big business. He cared about delighting users.

We loved all those things. So we paid $5 million in a mix of stock and cash. Tom also believed in us, so he took two-thirds in stock. He was bought-in and aligned.

• • •

ACQUISITIONS DONE MOSTLY IN STOCK ALIGN INCENTIVES WAY BETTER THAN CASH. CASH MEANS *THANK YOU, I'M OUT*. STOCK MEANS *I'M IN THIS WITH YOU*.

• • •

We changed the name to Streamlabs and reduced the fee from 1 percent to 0 percent, which increased growth. The strategy was to grow first and not try to build a business immediately; instead, use this as a wedge to build something bigger.

Tipping volume doubled each year over the next three years to $40 million, then $80 million, then $150 million a year. Our tipping and alerts tool became the most-used in the space.

DO MORE FOR THE SAME CUSTOMER

Omar was happy. We were relieved, vindicated—the *buy, then build* approach had worked. We had something real. So we did more acquisitions within the same space—building more for the same customer, live streamers. Becoming more essential to our users, a deeper part of their daily workflows, instinctively felt like the right way to grow.

Streamers were using all these tools to stream and make their career as a content creator:

- Tipping and alerts tools: to get donations, thank tippers, and encourage others to donate
- Streaming software: to capture, composite, and send video to Twitch
- Chatbots: to moderate spam and manage their chat
- Gamified widgets: progress bars, leaderboards, and so on, to encourage fans to donate or spend more
- Subscriptions: to get consistent support from fans each month
- Sponsors and ads: revenue that scaled with eyeballs, mostly from Twitch/YouTube
- Themes and widgets: to make their stream look more professional
- Merch: to sell T-shirts to fans, new revenue
- Mobile: to stream from their phones on-the-go, useful for in-real-life events
- Multi-stream: stream to multiple platforms at once, more audience
- Websites: hub for fans, showcase for brands
- Offline community: to run via chat on Discord
- Streaming platform: Twitch, YouTube, Facebook, or Mixer. A place to stream your content and build your following. Each had pros and cons, but Twitch was number one back then for live video.

We could do a lot more here. Some of these we built in-house, such as streamer websites. Some we acquired. Ankhbot was a popular chatbot that became part of Streamlabs. Our mobile streaming app, still the number one in the industry, was acquired from Adrian in Romania. Geoff and his team joined us to build merchandise stores for streamers. Trevor and StreamPro joined to build widgets and themes. We did four acquisitions, mostly in stock (lesson learned), and the founders joined to continue building with us.

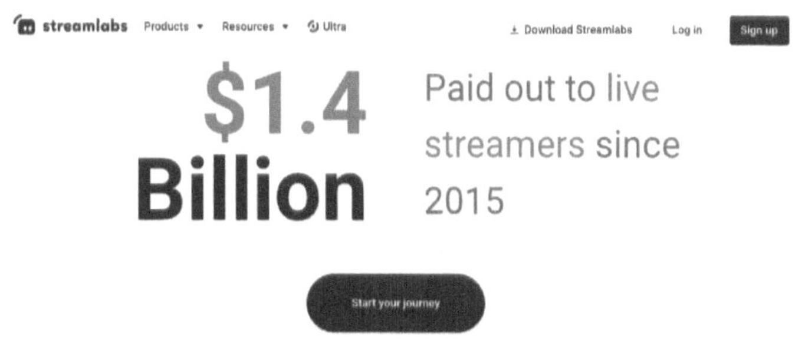

Streamlabs: Tipping, Alerts and Streaming Software

Murti: one of the things I'm proudest of is we treated these founders right, the way we ourselves would've liked to be treated by an acquirer. We gave them true ownership and agency over their products. All of the founders stayed with us for years, and many are still working at Streamlabs today a decade later.

One hundred percent of our traffic and users were from Twitch. This hadn't been a problem so far, but it worried us. As Andy Grove, the founder/CEO of Intel said (and titled his book) "Only the paranoid survive." If there was a policy change or Twitch decided to copy a feature in-house, that could become a huge problem. We started to build partnerships with You-Tube, Facebook, Mixer, TikTok, Instagram, and more. Many of them integrated us into their onboarding workflows for new streamers. They wanted a piece of the live video market that Twitch owned, and they saw working with Streamlabs as a way to get there.

HIRING THE RIGHT PEOPLE

Team offsite: Streamlabs in Napa

During this time, our tipping volume kept growing. We added a way for users to subscribe and get extra features (Pro effects) on their alerts. This brought in a few million in revenue. In our biggest year, we processed about $200 million in payments from fans to streamers in a single calendar year. From laying off everyone but a small team of 15, we grew back to 80 people.

Murti: We went deep and committed. With our mobile app, for example, to improve overheating and battery life, I put the phone in our fridge at the office and had it stream to test performance. I would stream my dog sleeping for 12 hours a day to optimize battery consumption.

We had six engineers on H-1B visas, which were expiring soon and needed to be renewed. Given how broken US skilled immigration was (and still is), most of them would not win the H-1B lottery to get a renewal and would have to go back to India, China, or Ukraine. Where else could we move these engineers?

I opened up Google Maps and zoomed out. Way out. Within our time zone, PST, a couple of options jumped out—Vancouver, Canada, and Mexico City, Mexico. Engineers were more excited about Canada. So I flew to Vancouver and set up our office there. Those six engineers moved to Vancouver. That office eventually grew to 40 people—all high-paying, six-figure, skilled jobs that the US lost.

. . .

ILLEGAL IMMIGRATION IS TOO EASY IN THE US; SKILLED, LEGAL IMMIGRATION IS TOO HARD. CANADA AND OTHER COUNTRIES ARE TAKING MUCH OF THIS TALENT.

. . .

Some of our best hires were founders who had previously failed. They brought founder energy. We were able to hire globally and bring them to Canada. We also had success hiring socially awkward or autistic people (more Tizz, not Rizz) who were often at a disadvantage in job interviews because they weren't good communicators. But on the job, they usually outperformed those who interviewed well. Generally speaking, the awkward ones are undervalued for reasons that have nothing to do with their actual skills.

Most companies run engineering top-down. Everyone reports to a CTO. Daily standups. Weekly check-ins. High in alignment. But this organization also kills speed. Any new idea has to crawl up and down the org chart for approval. At Streamlabs we did the opposite. We copied Spotify's pod model. Small teams of three or four owned a feature end to end. Total freedom. If they thought of something in the morning, they could ship it by afternoon. If they wanted to scrap it, they could. No approvals. No bottlenecks.

Murti: Salman was technically the CTO responsible for technical performance and decisions, but I people-managed the engineers. In practice all I did was clear the runway. An engineer would say, "Hey, here's an idea," and I'd say, "Cool, go try it." That was it. The org was flat, messy, and fast. It worked.

We hired George, a former professional poker player who ran biz-ops at Minecraft during their $2.5 billion sale to Microsoft. Ashray joined us from a large conglomerate. Both would go on to become leaders at Streamlabs. Harsha, Karl, Eric, Osama, Eric F., and Anastasia all joined us because they, too, were gamers and spent hours on Twitch watching our streamers. Years later, a Streamlabs "mafia" emerged—George, Eric, Osama, Oat, and Anfal are all tinkering and working on new startups themselves. These networks percolated and proliferated. We're

all grandkids and great-grandkids of Federal Telegraph, Shock-
ley, Fairchild Semiconductor, and HP.

Karl being Karl: painting a giant penis during a Paint Night for the team.

**THE PEOPLE WHO WORK AT STARTUPS EVENTUALLY
GO ON TO INVEST IN OR BUILD THEIR OWN STARTUPS.
THIS IS THE FOUNDATION OF SILICON VALLEY.**

It wasn't all smooth sailing. One of our competitors—a big content creator with a couple million followers—started trolling us. He made up lies: hidden fees, shady practices, whatever would stick. He broadcast them to his large audience on YouTube, and people believed him.

We could have ignored it. Instead, we got dragged into the mud. Online fights always look bad, and we looked like the bad guy: a corporation squeezing creators. We lost 5 percent of our customers. Some employees couldn't handle the online vitriol and quit. At conferences, people would glare at us like we were villains.

Ali: I got hate messages. Death threats. It was brutal. For two weeks I could barely work—I just hid and watched Netflix to survive. Each year a few startup founders commit suicide—now we understood why. Those months were some of the toughest personally.

We thought about suing our competitor. Everything he said was false. But lawsuits are a distraction. In the end, I told Murti, "If we're honest, do good work, and take care of our users, we'll stay in business. He won't. Fraud doesn't work in the long-run."

And that's what happened. He's gone now. We're not. What we learned was simple: Don't get pulled into fights with online trolls. Grow thick skin, put your head down, and keep building. The storm, however bad, will pass.

Kudos to Salman, Tom, Eric, Karl, Morgan, Chelsea, and our team that stood by us through it all. They showed character and resolve.

• • •

DON'T GET PULLED INTO FIGHTS WITH
ONLINE TROLLS. YOU'LL ALWAYS LOSE.

• • •

"GREAT JOB, WE'LL TAKE IT"

Ali: Things were humming along when one day we got an email from Emmett Shear, the CEO and co-founder of Twitch, asking to meet for coffee. We were excited—maybe Twitch was finally realizing the good work we were doing for their ecosystem. We could build a closer partnership or, at the very least, a personal relationship with the CEO.

"So I have some news," he started. "You've done a great job building out tipping. You're processing, what is it, $200 million a year?"

"Yep," I nodded.

"We're going to build tipping in-house as a platform feature. We think it's important for our users. It will be called Twitch Bits, and it's launching in six months."

I quietly sipped my coffee.

"This is a friendly heads-up. I'd suggest changing course and doing something else. Or you can, of course, compete with us."

It's all over, I thought as I walked back to our office.

I pulled Murti and Salman quietly into a conference room, not wanting everyone else to freak out. Instead of supporting their developer ecosystem, Twitch had taken the approach of copying us. We had built something on the Twitch platform that had become so popular that the platform itself decided to copy us.

Twitch had been acquired by Amazon for $1 billion a couple of years ago, and it felt like Amazon was turning the screws on them to make more money. This would absolutely wreck our payment volume. Most streamers would just use the built-in Twitch option, even if it was significantly worse.

Fuuuuccckkkk. What on Earth were we going to do next?

BUILDING REALLY HARD THINGS

We scrambled. We had a little cushion with all the different products we had built or acquired over the past year, but tipping was still our most-used product. The bigger the ship, the harder it is to change direction. We had just six months.

We experimented with building a payments network, becoming PayPal for gamers. Dead end. Then we got excited about interactive games on Twitch with Twitch Extensions—so excited we tried to build five games at once. All failed. We built a crypto-like coin for streamers and their fans called Super-MegaFan. All the crypto coins went from $0 to $20 per coin, then down back to $0. We tried expanding beyond Twitch: YouTube Live, Mixer, Facebook Live. It helped somewhat, but all the other platforms combined, for us at least, were smaller than Twitch.

Twitch copied other developers too. Michael Anderson and Eli Hooten built GameWisp so streamers could offer multiple subscription tiers. Twitch copied it and killed them. Michael from GameWisp, Ari from Maestro, others—they'd message us when it happened. We'd commiserate, gave each other shoulders to cry on, but there wasn't much else anyone could do.

The worst part: Twitch set the tone for the industry. If they built something, Facebook Live, YouTube Live, Mixer—everyone else copied it. Independent developers didn't just get shut out by Twitch. They got shut out everywhere.

The breakthrough came when we asked a simple question: what's absolutely essential to streaming? The answer was obvious: (1) a platform to stream to and (2) software to stream with. Everything else was optional.

At the time, everyone used OBS, which worked, but it felt like Linux—technically extremely powerful but clunky as hell. The interface looked like something from the '90s. Streamers weren't only using OBS. To go live, they juggled at least four windows: OBS for audio and video, Streamlabs for alerts, a chatbot for moderation, and a theme library for overlays. It was painful.

It reminded me of the first iPhone launch. Jobs said Apple was announcing three products: a phone, an iPod, and a web communicator. The audience thought he meant three devices. But really it was one. Apple just bundled three workflows into a single hit device.

That's what streamers wanted too. Not four different apps but one tool. With streaming, themes, alerts, and chatbots built-in. A unified workflow.

OBS was open source, which meant we didn't have to start from zero. We could build on top of it. So we did. We made a long-term bet on streaming software.

WHAT IS A PAINKILLER, AND WHAT IS A VITAMIN? WHAT IS ABSOLUTELY CRITICAL, AND WHAT IS OPTIONAL? IT'S A HELPFUL AND OBJECTIVE LENS TO SEE YOUR WORK.

Execution was rough. We didn't know C++, which was way harder than the web languages we were used to—PHP, Python, JavaScript. We tried hiring experts and open-source contributors, but none of them stuck.

Then Murti met Eddy Gharbi. On paper, Eddy had nothing: an F1 visa about to expire, no real dev experience. But he had what mattered—founder energy. He was a gamer, lived on Twitch, and was hungry. He promised a demo in a week. He delivered.

We paired Eddy with Andy (now Ava), another gamer and developer. Andy took the front end, Eddy the back end. The two of them worked mostly in isolation while the rest of the company doubted they'd ever ship. On weekends, Murti sat with them, streaming for eight hours at a time until the software stopped crashing. Slowly, we added themes, overlays, alerts.

We thought it would take three months. Eighteen months later, the software still wasn't done.

It was the hardest technical product we'd ever tried to build. Meanwhile, the rest of Streamlabs—the legacy business—was declining.

The board, employees, even Ali wasn't sure it would work. But Murti firewalled the OBS team—nicknamed SLOBS (Streamlabs OBS)—so they could grind without interference. They rewrote the code half a dozen times in C++ and Electron, refactoring the architecture over and over until it held.

**LONG-TERM PROJECTS REQUIRE FOCUS AND ISOLATION.
IF YOU DON'T SEPARATE THE TEAM, THEY'RE LIKELY TO
GIVE UP WHEN THEY DON'T SEE QUICK, EASY WINS.**

After 18 months, we finally had something better than OBS. To launch, we didn't overthink it. We put a download link in the top-left corner of our site and popped champagne on a Twitch stream. That was it. Millions clicked. Word spread. OBS users switched in droves.

Launching Streamlabs OBS at TwitchCon 2018

Every startup has two modes: pivot fast when things don't work or go deep when they do. The mistake is getting stuck in the middle. With Streamlabs OBS, we went very deep. We shut out distractions and focused only on the essential.

VC funding gave us the room to go deep. It also let us launch without worrying about a business model. Our bet was simple: if people loved the product, the business would come. And it did.

Suddenly, we weren't the same company anymore. New product. New direction.

At the time, no one had built a real business charging streamers directly. Platforms like Twitch, YouTube, and Facebook monetized fans. Other startups leaned on sponsors or subscriptions. Everyone assumed there weren't enough streamers to make them customers.

But with Streamlabs OBS, the streamers themselves *were* our customers. And there weren't thousands of them—there were tens of millions. Maybe this could work.

Streamlabs Prime—the streamer subscription—took years to find its footing. At first, we made the classic mistake of overestimating the short term. We added features we thought would be hits, like a website builder. Nobody cared. But themes and overlays? Streamers loved them. Then we opened an app store for third-party apps. Over time, the value stacked up.

Revenue growth was slow at first, but it compounded. Within a few years, Streamlabs Prime was pulling in $10 million in revenue, far more than our legacy product.

• • •

WHEN YOU FIND THE THING THAT REALLY MATTERS, PUT BLINDERS ON. GO ALL IN.

• • •

TWITCH STUDIO

On the back of this newfound traction, we raised a $20 million Series B round of funding with Michael Mullany from Icon Ventures. Turns out we would never use any of that money.

Our funding round generated some inbound acquisition interest from Corsair, the PC components manufacturer. They had already acquired Elgato and were selling directly to streamers and their fans. That got their competitors to take interest too—Logitech and Razer. Facebook and YouTube also looked at us strategically as a way to make inroads with streamers.

• • •

NOTHING GETS A LARGE COMPANY MORE INTERESTED IN PARTNERSHIPS OR MERGERS AND ACQUISITIONS THAN THEIR COMPETITORS ALSO BEING INTERESTED.

• • •

We weren't sure we wanted to sell. Omar, our board member from Sequoia, told us not to. "Moments like this are rare," he said. "You may never get back to a hundred-million-dollar scale." He was right. But I couldn't stop thinking about the $150 million DraftKings deal we'd passed on in 2015.

And then Twitch did what Twitch always does: copied us.

They announced Twitch Studio, a near clone of Streamlabs OBS. We felt like we were in that cartoon with two kids running from a bear. One says, "I don't have to outrun the bear, I just have to outrun you." Twitch was the bear. Developers like us were the kids. And Twitch never stopped running.

Ali: I shared this situation with another founder at Sequoia Basecamp. His advice was blunt: "Dude, *get the fuck out.*"

By then, we were exhausted. Nine years of building Streamlabs. Trolls. Pivots. Platform risk. Always running from the bear. When Twitch copied tipping, we swallowed it. When they copied the streaming software, it broke us.

Looking back, maybe we should have just taken a sabbatical—three months, six months, a year off. Maybe we would have come back with fresh energy and kept going. But in 2019, with the bear breathing down our neck, we were emotionally spent.

The lesson was simple: Building on someone else's platform is both the biggest opportunity and the biggest risk. The rules can change overnight. The platform can copy you and wipe you out. Treat it like rented land. Build just enough there to capture users, then move them onto your own product.

• • •

IF YOU'RE GOING TO PLAY THE PLATFORM GAME, YOU NEED A PLAN: GET BIG, GET FAST, AND GET OUT. USE THE PLATFORM AS A FUNNEL, NOT A FOUNDATION.

• • •

SELLING STREAMLABS

One of the first truths you learn about mergers and acquisitions: you can't sell a company. A company has to be bought. If it looks like you're shopping the company around, people assume something's wrong.

The best way to get bought is if your competitors want you.

For us, there were two groups of buyers. The first was the platforms: Twitch, YouTube, Facebook, Microsoft. Twitch was the obvious leader, but everyone else wanted to be. Buying Streamlabs could have been a way to catch up.

The second was hardware companies already selling to gamers: Logitech, Razer, Corsair. They were doing hundreds of millions in gear—mice, keyboards, webcams, lights, mics—and streamers were their target customer. For them, owning us meant owning that audience.

Ali: We explored both buckets. After our bad experience with bankers last time, I decided to run the process myself. The goal was simple: create competition. Talk to everyone, set deadlines, and get them bidding against each other.

Bucket one fizzled. Twitch didn't want to pay for users they already had. YouTube was lukewarm. Facebook came closest, but worried that if they bought us, Twitch would cut them off. They passed.

Bucket two was better. Razer offered a term sheet. Corsair showed interest. Logitech made a serious offer—cash, stock, and earnout—worth about $118 million at the time. That ended up being worth $170 million with their rising stock price.

The downside of not having a banker is that you have to be the bad guy yourself. You have to ask for more money and threaten to walk away. If you can't walk away, the deal won't close.

The Logitech deal took six months. We had to walk away more than once. The night before the press release announcing the deal, their lawyers raised last-minute tax issues. We told them no deal. Suddenly, the tax issues weren't an issue anymore.

Even after signing the term sheet, the final close kept dragging. Finally I called them and said, "If this isn't done by Monday, we're out. Our revenues are growing. The price is already outdated. We can't keep doing this dance."

They were shocked. "You're going to walk away? We already announced the deal. Can't you just wait another week?"

No, after six months of deal diligence, we couldn't and we wouldn't. They ultimately agreed.

I burned some relationships here. But that's the cost of running your own process. If you want to close without a banker, you'll piss some important people off. And then you'll still have to work with them the next day.

The day we announced the deal, the Logitech execs came to our San Francisco office early in the morning. Most of the team had no idea. At 9:00 a.m., we called an all-hands, dialed in Vancouver, and shared the news as the press release went out.

There was excitement. Questions too—about next steps, jobs, the future. Everyone got a raise. It was the biggest financial transaction of our lives. I thought I'd feel joy. Instead, all I felt was relief.

Relief that the long, painful journey was over. Relief that we hadn't died. Relief that we could *just stop worrying*. After taking punch after punch through countless pivots, we were just glad to have landed the plane safely.

WHEN THE MAGIC'S GONE

The moment a deal starts moving, people change. Money flips a switch. Suddenly it's not about the mission anymore—it's *what's in it for me?* You can feel the magic draining before the ink is dry.

Everyone on the team made money—on average, six figures. Andy, who'd been through five startups before, said, "This is the first time my equity actually turned into something. That's cool." But others chafed. Some thought they deserved more. Some had negotiated cash instead of equity and now resented it. That's how it always goes.

Our angels were ecstatic. Many 10X'd their money. They sent thank-you notes, calls, letters. Sequoia made a 4X cash return in four years. We barely got a nod or thank-you. As founders you risk everything, and even when you deliver, the VCs hardly care. It felt so shitty. The contrast between angels and VCs couldn't have been more stark.

Murti: When Logitech bought us, we were told we'd report to the CEO. Instead, we got shuffled under someone else. We were promised autonomy. P&L control. Freedom to run the business. The next day, that promise was gone. We were expected to hit revenue targets but couldn't decide how to spend. Employee raises were capped at 3 percent annually—less than inflation. You can't keep great people in a software company that way.

The dysfunction piled up. Our Vancouver office was full of immigrant engineers we'd worked hard to bring in from Europe. They were loyal but vulnerable. Their visas had to be transferred quickly or they'd be invalid. HR didn't understand immigration, didn't see the urgency. I warned them these engineers might leave. Instead of fixing it, they reprimanded me for "speaking that way" to HR. I was furious. They'd just spent $170 million on this team, and now they were bungling the people and the paperwork. That's the kind of thing that kills founder energy.

Ali: Before the deal, a friend, Julian from Elgato, had warned me, "Logitech's culture is toxic. You won't like it." I brushed it off. *Every big company has problems,* I thought. *We'll survive.* But he was right.

Murti: When the deal closed, I wanted to stay four or five years. I'd already hit my personal number. Everything else was going to charity. I was happy to just keep building. Day two, I knew it wasn't going to work. I wanted to quit on the spot. Ali talked me down into vesting-in-peace.

We just had to stay nine months and keep revenue steady to unlock our earnout. We did. When that period ended, Logitech didn't even try to keep us. They spent $170 million on us, and they just didn't care whether the founders stayed or left. It was nuts.

That was fine. We were ready to leave.

After we left, Streamlabs caught the Covid wave. In 2021, every online platform surged as people were stuck at home.

Better to be lucky than smart. Revenue jumped from $15 million to over $50 million almost overnight.

Years later, tens of millions of streamers still use Streamlabs. Just this week, Ashray from Streamlabs went up on stage at MetaConnect to announce a livestreaming partnership for their new Meta RayBan glasses. We didn't leave behind a lemon. We left behind a real company. It's bittersweet leaving, but we're proud we built something real. Tizz, not just Rizz.

We'll bleed Streamlabs forever.

CHAPTER 9

STONKS

When we sold Peanut Labs, we didn't make that much for six years of work—about $1 million each. Half went to buy our mom a house, the rest to taxes. Then we jumped straight into the next startup. No pause.[5]

Streamlabs was different. The exit was life-changing. Enough money that we never had to work again. We each bought a house for the first time. But beyond that, life stayed the same. Same food, same clothes, same cars. The big change wasn't money—it was time.

The problem is, people who build companies can't sit still. Give us too much free time and we go nuts. We need something hard to push against.

Murti: A year after the sale, I moved to Southern California and became a surfer bum. Surfed four or five times a week. Played squash. Told myself I was done with startups. At the same time, Ali, Cassius, Gauher, and I started a nonprofit called Pledges to fund coding bootcamps for needy students around the world.

The traditional narrative around poverty and opportunity suggests that if someone is born poor, in a third-world country, or without resources, the missing piece is simply access to training and tools. Provide the resources, and people transform their lives.

So we designed courses and offered them free of charge to 15,000 students. These weren't amateur efforts. The courses were conducted by professional institutes in local classroom settings equipped with the latest technology and equipment, designed to give people tools to upskill and get higher-paying jobs. We literally spoon-fed students. All they had to do was finish the courses and apply for a job, and they'd be on their way to improving their family situations.

Yet over half the people who started dropped out before even finishing the course. Many who did complete the training didn't continue practicing their skills and never went out to get a job—which was the whole point of the program.

What we learned was that most people are lazy, regardless of who they are or where they come from. Even when provided with everything they need to succeed, the majority won't put in the effort required to change their circumstances.

That's a harsh conclusion, but the data doesn't lie. The problem isn't always a lack of resources or opportunity—sometimes it's simply a lack of motivation to do the work, even when the path to success is clearly laid out and fully supported.

After three years, we pivoted the nonprofit to help with humanitarian causes instead.

MORA MEDICAL

Murti: Around the time I was working on Pledges, my mom came to visit me in California. At that point, she was on six or seven meds—blood pressure, blood sugar, the usual. I put her on a whole-food, plant-based diet—salads and smoothies—and had her walk an hour a day. Within weeks her blood sugar normalized. She stopped all her meds. It was like magic.

Ali and I had been into clean eating for years, so I knew it worked. But seeing it happen so fast made me think: *This is worth a company. This is worth coming out of retirement for.*

So, in 2022, I teamed up with Eddy from Streamlabs as CTO, and Laurie, a vegan doctor and lifestyle medicine physician, as our medical cofounder. We raised $6 million. Since medicine is regulated state by state, Laurie got licensed in all 50 states, and we created five local LLC entities in different states. We figured out how to get insurance to cover it.

The model was group medical visits. Patients with chronic conditions—mostly diabetes and heart disease—would see Laurie or one of our other doctors once a week, together with seven or eight other patients. We billed insurance, so it was free to them.

Sadly, we ran into a situation like the one we experienced with Pledges: even when high-quality help is provided for free, people don't take advantage of it. They're not willing to change their behavior.

One of our doctors was a cardiac surgeon in Texas. His patients were typically older and overweight with a history of poor lifestyle choices—eating junk food and red meat, smoking, not exercising—that ultimately led to a heart attack. After operating on patients to repair the damage and insert a stent, the cardiologist would send patients to a Mora nurse located in the same office. The nurse would talk to patients about next steps: "Hey, now that you've had surgery, let's put some preventative care in place so this doesn't happen to you again."

The response? Many patients laughed it off. Even those who began the protocol stopped within a week or two. They started smoking again and kept eating red meat. They had just had a heart attack, but they were unwilling to change their eating habits—even if those changes could potentially save their life.

As with Pledges, I became discouraged and, after two years, shut Mora down.

• • •

THE HARDEST THING TO CHANGE IS PEOPLE'S HABITS AND CORE BEHAVIORS. PEOPLE DON'T FUNDAMENTALLY CHANGE.

• • •

STONKS 1.0

Ali: While Murti moved to Southern California, I stayed in Northern California. At first, my wife was happy when I was done with Streamlabs, but I struggled with not having a real problem or direction to work on. I moped around, doing random things—Netflix, video games, and spending time with kids. Eventually, my wife said, "I think you should just go back to work. You're just better off when you're working."

So in early 2021, a year after leaving Streamlabs, I started tinkering. I liked working with founders, so I hosted a weekly Shark Tank–style show on Clubhouse where founders pitched live to VCs. The show immediately took off: after one session, investors wired $200,000 to founders. We were on to something.

The team built a platform around this called Stonks—live-streamed startup demo days. Raised $19 million in funding. It was like Twitch and Angellist had a baby. After suffering at the hands of Twitch, I wanted to build a live-video platform of my own in a different vertical.

Investors could one-click request an intro, sign SAFE docs, pool and wire funds in an SPV (special purpose vehicle), and close the deal all from within the Stonks platform. Startup accelerators like Techstars, 500, Snapchat, Draper, Hustle Fund, Plug & Play, Capital Factory, Xoogler, and others already hosted in-person demo days. They approached us to ask, "Can we host our demo days on this platform too?"

Yes, why not. So we started adding partner demo days to the platform in addition to our own.

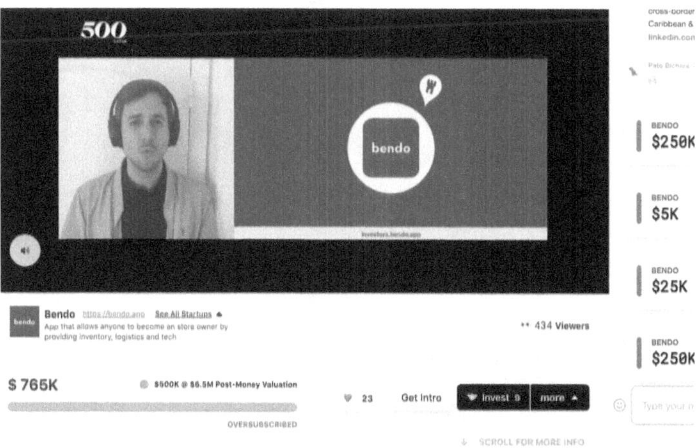

Stonks Demo Days: bringing Silicon Valley together to invest during COVID-19.

On one of our demo days, investors tuned in to see the usual cast of characters—founders pitching, John (my co-founder) and myself hosting, and VCs judging. But there was someone else, a familiar face.

Curly, overgrown hair.

Stoner face.

The swagger of a hotshot founder. All Rizz, no Tizz.

It was Erlich Bachmann, the hacker house founder from HBO's TV show *Silicon Valley.*

The founders were stunned. VCs erupted in howls. Chat on the livestream went wild. People started screenshotting this and putting it on X/Twitter.

"So what dogshit idea are you pitching to me today?" Erlich said to the founders.

And "These pitches smell worse than human excrement."

And "Are you drinking your own Kool-Aid, or do you just expect to scam us?"

One of the VC panelists actually fell off his chair. Really. This was the sequel to *Silicon Valley* that the people deserved.

. . .

MAKE WORK FEEL LIKE PLAY. IF YOU HAVE FUN WITH IT, YOUR CUSTOMERS WILL TOO.

. . .

John and Olivier with Erlich Bachmann from HBO's Silicon Valley.

In 2022 Stonks hosted 157 online demo day events; 1,500 startups pitched, and they raised over $100 million in investments—our best year.

Stonks and Clubhouse were where Silicon Valley hung out, did deals, and networked during COVID-19. We were feeling so bullish that we even acqui-hired OnePager, a startup in our space that was shutting down. Adam, Jack, and Nick joined the team.

Then COVID-19 ended.

Y Combinator and others returned to in-person. Online demo days turned from painkiller to vitamin. Behavior normalization hit other pandemic companies too—Zoom, Peloton, Hopin, and others saw their stocks drop 90 percent or more.

The founder and CEO of US Mobile, one of the best startups on Stonks, called me and said, "Ali, I want to raise from you guys, but I don't want to pitch hundreds of random investors online. I'd rather raise in private."

We had moved hundreds of millions from investors to startups. But post-COVID-19, the best founders didn't want to raise online. You can't build a fundraising platform without the best founders. The model broke.

It sucked balls, but it was time to pivot.

PRIVATE MARKET INVESTING

Ali: In early 2023, our team did rapid experimentation, launching:

- TurboTax for Angels: a tax software for startup investors that used QSBS (Qualified Small Business Stock) and tax-loss harvesting to reduce your tax bill.
- Startup Portfolio AI: automating the task of collecting

founder updates using AI from all the startups in your portfolio.
- Hiring Demo Days: startup job fairs
- Reverse Demo Days: VCs pitching to founders, instead of vice versa
- SaaS Tooling for accelerators
- Y Combinator for bootstrapped founders

The TurboTax for startup investors was the first time we used Claude and ChatGPT to code and navigate tax law. It was magical—we had 95 percent of the accuracy of an expert CPA in seconds, for free. And we could prototype 100X faster.

Olivier (my technical co-founder) and I silo-ed ourselves away from the rest of the team, went to a co-working space, and put our heads down. For reference, it takes Intuit a year and hundreds of engineers to just push an *update* to TurboTax. We built something in three weeks.

That was when I started to realize that AI was a game changer for coding, research, and deep-knowledge work.

All these ideas had some revenue but ultimately didn't work—too niche of a market, hard user acquisition, poor unit economics, or something else. We had, however, assembled a valuable audience of over 100,000 startup investors, half of whom were accredited.

Our quantitative testing data showed that these investors all wanted to invest in OpenAI, SpaceX, Stripe, Anthropic, and other hot late-stage pre-IPO deals. Investing in late-stage, pre-IPO startups was basically impossible if you weren't writing a million-dollar-plus check. So we built and launched several iterations of Sandhill Markets, an investing platform that aimed to democratize access into pre-IPO startups for angel investors.

We tested different approaches to get small investors into

big deals, including annual subscriptions, tradeable SPV interests, Series SPVs. Our testing data was correct; there was real demand. Our existing audience quickly paid, and Sandhill Markets grew to $500,000 ARR in a month.

But new user acquisition was a huge problem. Paid channels were running at $4,000 plus per paid customer. That wouldn't work. How were we going to grow?

I've always loved auctions. They're the beating heart of any market. Wall Street itself started in the 1800s as a weekly auction of shares, held in a small office on Wall Street.

Live auctions felt like the right way to fix our growth problem. They're exciting, social, and transparent. And they could be done on live video, like WhatNot or eBay Live.

With AI, our team built the system in three weeks. We borrowed best practices from Nasdaq and NYSE, and gave bidders funny animal names—*Ambulatory Orangutan, Nervous Kookaburra, Eager Tortoise.*

We ran auctions for stakes in Flexport, Epic Games, SpaceX, Mercury, Stripe—blue-chip pre-IPO startups. The last hour of each auction was a livestream show. Adam (my main deal guy) and I would host with a guest—Eric Ries from LTSE (Long-Term Stock Exchange), for example—while cheering on bidders as they went head-to-head.

It wasn't quite Erlich Bachmann roasting founders on Stonks, but it was close. Maybe more exciting, because nobody knew where the auction stock price would end up.

When we auctioned Mercury, Mercury employees shared it in their company Slack. Everyone wanted to see what the market thought their shares—and by extension, their net worth—were worth. It's natural human behavior.

Another favorite moment in building Sandhill was when Elon Musk was buying Twitter. Investors wanted in. We organized an unauthorized fan "protest" at the Tesla factories in Austin, Texas, and Fremont, California, to petition Elon Musk to let us invest in his buyout of Twitter.

Security showed up at the protest in Fremont and asked me, "What are you doing here?"

"We're the Elon Musk fan club," I said, thinking on my feet.

Security couldn't possibly kick out their boss' fan club and hope to keep their jobs.

It worked! Security left us alone. And we got access to the Twitter/X.com deal for our investors.

The "Elon Musk Fan Club" at Tesla Fremont

But SpaceX and other companies sent us cease-and-desist notices. They didn't want a horde of small checks in their mega-rounds. We were on the hitlist of General Counsels and legal teams everywhere.

My friend, the founder and CEO of Mercury, called me

and said, "Ali, I've got legal and marketing breathing down my neck telling me to stop this. They don't want random investors buying shares." That was the final nail.

There was a fundamental misalignment of incentives here: Successful pre-IPO companies did not want lots of small investors in their deals because they could potentially mess things up. But those were the very companies that angel investors really wanted to invest in.

In one extreme example, we had a small angel investor with a $10,000 check blow up a $20 million allocation into OpenAI because the investor didn't wire funds on time and then complained to the SEC and to OpenAI about being left out. OpenAI canceled the entire $20 million deal—the hassle wasn't worth it for them. It was easier and less annoying to just sell that $20 million to a VC fund.

In hindsight, it's obvious why late-stage startups don't want to deal with hundreds of small investors. Democratizing investing didn't work here.

• • •

WHEN CUSTOMER AND STAKEHOLDER INCENTIVES DON'T ALIGN, IT'S A VERY UPHILL BATTLE BUILDING A BUSINESS.

• • •

Shout-out to both Adams, Olivier, Eric, Derek (RIP), and Jonathan here; Sandhill couldn't have happened without you.

After OpenAI cancelled the $20 million deal, I had had enough. We spun-off the Sandhill brand and assets to Adam, and he continues to manage LPs and runs it as a fund instead. We laid off the rest of the team except Olivier and myself. We had some good people, and as a solo-founder, this really hit me hard. It was painful—despite customers, $500,000 ARR, and PMF, we had to pivot again.

STONKS 2.0: RETURN OF THE JEDI

Ali: Stonks had raised a large seed round of $19 million during the 2021 bubble, and $11 million of that was still in the bank. My instinct was familiar: buy small companies that already had PMF, then scale them. Buying to get to PMF is underrated. We scanned hundreds of deals in AI, SaaS, and creator tools—but nothing passed. Either the business wasn't right, or the price wasn't right.

Then the floor fell out from under me. Olivier—our CTO—didn't want to buy anything. He got bored easily; he couldn't stick to one thing. One day he Slack-messaged, "I'm out." We had just laid off the whole team. Now my CTO quit. I was suddenly very, very alone.

I told myself I was fine. My wife said, "Are you sure you're ok?"

"Yeah, I'm fine. I'll get over it," I said. I thought I was fine.

My body said *fuck no*. Years of arthritis, an autoimmune condition I'd been managing, flared badly. Chronic stress and the feeling of being abandoned pushed it over the edge: meds stopped working, joints got worse. Doctors couldn't fix it. I was getting worse by the day. My body was saying, *stop, just stop*.

I nearly shut the whole thing down.

Then Murti came back. He'd shut down Mora Medical and was bored. I asked him to join Stonks. He said yes. We had money, and he needed a challenge. Eddy Almeida from Mora returned as CTO. Getting the old team back changed everything. I didn't have to carry it alone. Multiple pivots bleed you dry; doing them solo is nigh impossible. With Murti and Eddy back, the pressure eased, and the startup lived another day.

. . .

IF YOU'RE GOING TO PIVOT, DON'T DO IT WITHOUT CO-FOUNDERS. JUST DON'T.

. . .

Stonks 2.0 team, left to right: Ali, Eddy, Carl, Murti, Ludo, Seda, Caden

We'd always wanted to try "Twitch for Investing"—investors discussing and trading the stock market live on-air. Stonks 2.0 was exactly that and launched in summer 2024. It grew fast. Thousands of daily users. A small, tight-knit community of day-traders formed. We even had public-company CEOs (like Nasdaq: WAVE) come on for live interviews.

Earnings calls became a natural magnet for viewers to get together.

The format worked perfectly for day-trading stocks and crypto. The problem was, neither of us are day-traders. More than that, we're against it. Day-trading is a losing game—over 90 percent of traders lose money. And what we'd built wasn't really "Twitch for Investing." It was "Twitch for Day-Trading."

We didn't want to be drug dealers, pushing something we thought was harmful to retail investors. *Do no harm.*

Time to pivot.

MORA 2.0

Ali: It was August 2024. I asked ChatGPT, "How do I save and invest for my kids tax-free? How do I take care of them if my startup doesn't work?"

Among other things, ChatGPT suggested Roth IRAs for Kids. Adults put post-tax money into a Roth so they won't be taxed when they take distributions. Why not do the same with kids: give them a job, pay them wages, let them pay taxes now, and then let the money saved grow for 50 years. A quick Google search showed that thousands of families were already doing this. Murti and I checked with our lawyer and CPA and learned it could work if structured correctly.

So we launched our Roth IRA for Kids under the Mora brand. We became an RIA (Registered Investment Advisor), passed the Series 65 exam, and partnered with Charles Schwab to establish FDIC/SIPC-insured accounts.

In four months we went from "Twitch for Gambling Day-Traders" to a regulated RIA, serving long-term ROTH IRA retirement accounts for families and kids.

One of the hardest parts of doing a Roth for Kids yourself

is that parents have to run payroll through a payroll processor, create an employment agreement with their children, keep pay stubs and time logs, create W-2s at the end of the year, and so on. It was painstakingly cumbersome and manual.

Our value proposition was that we automated the process. Friends, family, and Stonks users loved it. Many Stonks investors became customers themselves so they could save millions for their kids tax-free.

But new customer acquisition was excruciatingly slow—six months and 10-plus touchpoints before new users became customers. Customers had to trust we'd be around in 40 years for their kids. But we still believed. The foundation of tax-savings was solid.

Then in early 2025, President Trump introduced the "big beautiful tax bill" that included a new type of account specifically for kids with a free $1,000 from the government. No complicated lock-ups or eligibility rules like the Roth IRA. Eighty percent of the benefit for a lot less work. Great for the country, bad for us.

We tested another version of Mora that was more focused on estate-planning, but the CAC/LTV (Customer Acquisition Cost/Lifetime Value) numbers didn't work as soon as we scaled up marketing spend to anything significant.

We had to pivot again.

STONKS 3.0—FOR CREATORS

Ali: One of the big lessons from Mora was that people *love* keeping more of the money they earn—legally. Tax optimization sounds boring, but saving thousands a year hits differently when it's your own money.

While playing around with a Roth IRA for Kids, Murti

discovered a tax strategy that could help creators—streamers, YouTubers, influencers. We'd spent a decade in that world. So we combined what we knew and built **Stonks 3.0**, a product that helped creators save an average of $8,000 a year by running their work like a business—tracking expenses, organizing receipts, and deducting them properly.

We didn't invent anything new. The IRS already had an 11-point checklist for independent contractors. We just automated it.

The hardest part in fintech isn't building the product—it's getting people to care. Distribution costs more than development. Luckily, we'd spent years building relationships across the creator economy. That gave us a head start on partnerships and go-to-market.

We decided to launch at TwitchCon 2025, just like we did with Streamlabs years ago. Murti, Caden, Eddy, and the team went all-in. We built a flashy booth with a giant spin-the-wheel cash game. Creators could win real money—instantly deposited into their new Stonks account. We gave away high-quality merch: backpacks, jackets, phone wallets. No cheap swag.

The booth crushed. Long lines. Over 1,000 creators opened Stonks accounts in three days.

The Stonks booth at TwitchCon '25

Then we talked to them.

"Taxes? Uh, I don't really know what to do with that," most said. They weren't interested in saving on taxes—they just wanted free money. We realized we were selling college courses to fifth graders.

By day three, it was clear: This wasn't going to work. The team looked exhausted.

That's when Murti had a simpler idea. "What if we just get creators their YouTube money faster?"

YouTube pays out 45–60 days after ad earnings. What if we advanced that money in seven days or less?

Eddy and Carl spun up a landing page. Murti ran some Meta ads. Within hours, users started signing up. Then more.

Within a week, we hit a $1 million ARR run-rate. Profitably.

Holy shit.

. . .

THE SIMPLER SOMETHING IS, THE BETTER IT WORKS.

. . .

Our developers had to mute the Slack channel that pings for every new subscriber. Too many dings.

Andrew Chen at a16z calls this *selling chocolate instead of broccoli*—give people what they crave, not what they need.

Our Roth for Kids needed a 140 IQ to understand. Taxes for Creators was a 120 IQ product. Get Your YouTube Earnings Fast is an 80 IQ product. Funny how that's the one that worked best.

As of this writing, we've been running this latest idea for two weeks. We've seen promising starts die before, so we're cautious. It'll take months to know if this one's real.

Still—this feels like one of the most promising beginnings we've ever had.

ONE MORE THING...

We wanted to end this book on a high. On finding PMF. On getting to the promised land. We really did.

But when has anything ever gone according to plan?

The new product to get YouTube earnings fast looked perfect on paper: $99 a year, plus a 3 percent fee on advances. We could acquire paying users for $15 each through Meta ads. They got a 30-day free trial that required a credit card.

Pay $15, get $99. Infinite money glitch.

Free trials usually have some churn—maybe 35 percent. But around 65 percent stick. That's the math every SaaS founder knows.

Then we tried to charge the cards. Ninety-seven percent failed. Error: *Insufficient Funds.*

What the fuck?

In 20 years of building startups, we had never seen anything like that. We dumped the data into ChatGPT and asked what was happening. "You're not being scammed," it said. "The Meta algorithm is optimizing for what you asked for—users who put in a credit card for a free trial."

It turns out there's an entire shadow population online— millions of people with credit cards that have exactly $1 on them. Just enough to pass a free trial. Not enough to ever pay. They sign up for Netflix, Spotify, whatever, rinse, repeat.

Meta found them for us. At scale.

Our $15 CAC (customer acquisition cost) wasn't real.

By Monday, the success we thought we'd found had evaporated. Thousands of "paying" users—none real.

So much for ending on a high.

No happily ever after. This is real startup life. Taking punches right up to the end.

Most products die. Most founders lose. All we can do is reset and try to find the strength to keep going.

The search continues.

. . .

STARTUPS DON'T DIE WHEN THEY RUN OUT OF MONEY; THEY DIE WHEN FOUNDERS RUN OUT OF OPTIMISM.

—DALTON CALDWELL, Y COMBINATOR, STANDARD CAPITAL

. . .

TL;DR

By definition, decision making is hard; startups are hard. Don't expect it to be easy. We both suffer from chronic stress-related health issues that get worse with startups—Murti has migraines, Ali has arthritis. Our Slack directory looks like a ghostly cemetery with 100 names in grey (past team members) and only a handful still active, a testament to the human cost of pivoting.

Still, you must remain flexible and open to pivoting. Too many founders stick with their original idea, never adapting or changing, until the bitter end. It's a more dangerous sin to stick with an idea too long than to pivot too early.

How do you know when it's time to pivot? Knowing that answer is art and science. Math and madness. The most elegant way to answer is to ask yourself, "Am I still optimistic about what I'm doing? Do I still feel energized to keep going?"

If you as the founder are not genuinely optimistic and haven't been for a while, it's probably time to pivot.

Give yourself another shot on goal. And another. And another, if that's what it takes.

Just don't stop shooting.

TAKE OUR ENERGY

The gaming meme at the beginning of this book is why we wrote this book:

┌ つ ●_● ┐つ ┌ つ ●_● ┐つ ┌ つ ●_● ┐つ┌ つ ●_● ┐つ

We want you to take our energy, gain inspiration from our failures, and just keep on going. We want you to win. It's not over until you, and you alone, say it's over. We want you to understand that you're not alone. What you're experiencing—starting, building, pivoting, failing, pivoting, failing, pivoting—is par for the course. Crazy things happen, sometimes outside of your control—layoffs, industry changes, legal problems, and more. Sure, we succeeded in that we sold two companies, but we spent *a lot* of time failing in between. And we're still *mostly failing* with our third startup. Startups are not linear; they are filled with ups and downs, false starts and mistakes.

As our stories show, we never finished the way we started. You'll get there, whatever "there" looks like. Just don't give up. Live another day. Take another shot on goal.

We learned with each failure and pivot. We said we wouldn't make this a how-to book, but it's impossible to resist creating a handy Top 7 list.

How to not give up:

1. Self-care: Seven to eight hours of sleep, healthy food, regular exercise, regular intimacy (however you define that).
2. Co-founders: Don't do it alone. Have one or more co-founders.
3. Purpose: care deeply about the problem emotionally, irrationally.

4. Pivot: Be flexible if it's not working and you're no longer optimistic.
5. Desperation: Burn the boats. You need this startup to work. No plan B.
6. Speed: More shots on goal.
7. Energy: Be irrationally optimistic. Optimism is infectious. Your first 20 hires should only be optimistic people.

Our Top 7 list is roughly in the order of importance. Start at the top and work your way down until all seven are part of your regular routine.

THE SHIT LIST SCORECARD

So, now that you've read about all the dumb shit we did and still survived, it's your turn. Let's play a game.

Every founder has battle scars. But how do you know if you've *really earned* your spot in the Startup Trauma Hall of Fame? Answer these 25 deeply uncomfortable, tragically common questions. Each "yes" earns you one point. Some questions earn you more. Tally your score, cry quietly in the shower, then compare notes with other masochists over La Croix in your co-working space. No cheating. Posting on Twitter/X is mandatory or it never happened: #MyShitScore.

Remember: therapy is optional; bullshit is mandatory.

THE SHIT LIST SCORECARD

1. Have you had a co-founder breakup?
2. Has an investor ghosted you harder than your Tinder matches?
3. Have you ever been down to less than three months' runway and told the team it was "strategic lean mode"?
4. Has an employee quit and taken half your codebase with them (and maybe your office coffee machine)?
5. Have you been sued by someone who used to smile at you in meetings?
6. Did your "viral launch" get fewer likes than your mom's birthday post?
7. Have you raised a round only to immediately realize your burn was double what you thought?
8. Has your AWS bill ever exceeded your revenue?
9. Have you ever signed a terrible deal just to "get the logo on the slide deck"?
10. Have you been rejected by Y Combinator? More than once? (1 point for each YC rejection)
11. Have you had to explain to your board why you hired your roommate as Head of Growth? Or your ex as Head of People?
12. Has a VC stolen your pitch deck and invested in a competitor?
13. Has a "strategic partner" ghosted you right after making you fly cross-country?
14. Has your VC ever told you that you were a disappointment?
15. Have you had to lay people off and then bump into them at Trader Joe's?
16. Did your "world-changing" app ever get a 1-star review that simply said "scam"?
17. Have you ever pivoted so hard you basically became a completely different company? (1 point for each complete 180-degree pivot.)

18. Have you lost a significant other who asked you to pick between them or the startup? (1 point for each occurrence)

19. Have you lost money to "friends and family" who now won't invite you to Thanksgiving?

20. Has a "beta test" accidentally gone live on Product Hunt?

21. Have you had an intern or engineer accidentally delete production data?

22. Have you ever taken three meetings with a VC associate who promised to introduce you to their partner but never did?

23. Have you been rejected by so many VCs that you can rank them by the quality of receptionists?

24. Did you once celebrate a "term sheet" that evaporated 72 hours later?

25. Have you considered moving to Bali or Dubai to become a "solopreneur" at least once this year?

RESULTS: WHAT YOUR SHIT-LIST SCORE SAYS ABOUT YOU

0—6: Fresh Meat

Congrats, rookie. You still think "runway" means airplanes. Enjoy the optimism while it lasts—reality will find you.

7—14: Mildly Traumatized

You've seen some things. Enough to have a Medium post about "lessons learned," not enough to get a book deal like us. Keep grinding.

15—21: Certified Masochist

You wake up in cold sweats, but investors call it "grit." Your LinkedIn humblebrags hide a thousand silent screams. People buy you coffee just to hear your war stories.

22—25+: Full PTSD Unicorn Whisperer

You've unlocked the secret level of startup hell. Every scar is a case study, every disaster a keynote. The bad news: you're permanently broken. The good news: Andreessen just offered you $50 million.

0—6: Fresh Meat

Once you're done, post your score on X/Twitter with the hashtag #MyShitScore. We'll find you and commiserate together.

HELP SOMEONE ELSE SURVIVE

Did you like this book? One final action item, perhaps the most important: Share the book with another founder who needs some encouragement and inspiration. Give our founder energy and these stories to someone else who's struggling, doubting, on the verge of quitting. Maybe they won't give up. Maybe they'll take one more shot on goal, and maybe they'll make it. And they'll thank you for it.

We love talking to and helping founders. Come find us on X/Twitter at @ali_moiz and @mecolalu.

ACKNOWLEDGMENTS

Our editing and publishing team at Scribe:

Lindsey and Gail—for helping put our story into words, editing, and keeping us moving with deadlines. This book wouldn't have happened otherwise.

Michael—for a lovely cover illustration. The arrows going everywhere capture the sense of chaos. Ami—for the back cover and description.

Jamie—for keeping us on track overall with publishing milestones.

Those who were in the trenches with us:

Zaki—for starting our very first internet venture building websites in the '90s, running Xuqa, jamming strategy over hookah, so many parties, and connecting us to great founders like Misbah at Jar. Our holding company is named after Gaming Ventura, where it all began. You're the first OG.

Jazz and Wei—for jamming on startups with us at Williams College.

Noman (Nomi) and Prosper—for all the sacrifices, pivots, resets from zero that went into building HotCampusParties, iVentster, Xuqa, and Peanut Labs. For giving up market salaries, becoming co-founders, and trusting us with your careers. For taking on bigger technical challenges than you knew how to solve and doing them anyway.

Rahil, Saad (Saadullah), Salman, Dan Gailey, Eddy Gharbi, Eddy Almeida, Andy (Ava), Morgan, Oat, Geoff, Andrew, Osama, Eric, Carl, Karl, Harsha, Adrian, and Marcin—for being brilliant developers, PMs, designers and technical leaders that took on tough, intractable problems. Whether it was learning to code in C++ for Streamlabs OBS, scaling to 1 billion+ API calls per day, or throwing away your prototypes each time we pivoted, you guys kept it all together. This wouldn't have been possible without your faith and trust.

Sean, Matt, Anya, Ed, Courtney, and John—for making it rain with clients and partners. You helped us find early customers, land important deals, and create buzz. Startups are equal parts selling and building, but building usually gets all the headlines.

Aaron, Marilyn, Nirman, Jared, Julia, and Caden—for being our favorite interns. It's been a source of un-ending joy and pride watching you grow into VPs, managers and directors, now leading your own teams forward. Remember to give back, and pay it forward in what you do.

George and Ashray—for helping us build and run Streamlabs, growing into kind, thoughtful leaders, and keeping the legacy going even after we left. You helped us hire, manage, and operate day-to-day. You will go on to do great things, and this is just the beginning.

John, Davis, Courtney, Adam, Jack, Nick, Matt, Olivier, Jeremy, Antoan, Joaquin, Celento, and Eric—for the crazy journey that was Stonks, Sandhill, and more. Thirteen pivots (and counting). It was a joy building and working with you during the Covid years. We brought Silicon Valley together when everyone was stuck at home.

Gauher, Sanam, and Cassius—for helping run Pledges, our non-profit foundation, and keeping us sane managing all of the crazy investing we've done. We've signed on to the founders' pledge to give away most of what we've made during our lifetimes.

Mike Sego—for being the first partner for Peanut Labs with Fluff Friends.

Diego—for CSGOJackpot. It didn't work, but we tried together.

Tom Maneri—for trusting us with your baby, TwitchAlerts. It's hard to build something users want, and it's even harder to let it go. Your trust was the foundation for Streamlabs. We hope we've done everything you expected, and more.

Chris, Kushagra, Leonard, Rene, Elizabeth, Maria, and David—for being early believers and partners in our Demo Day platform (Stonks 1.0).

Laurie, Tom, Shaleen, Eddy, and the many doctors who helped fund and build plant-based medical clinic Mora.com— for helping patients heal by changing their core habits. It didn't work out, but we tried.

Those who enabled us with capital, trust, mentorship:

Mark Gold—for being the very first person to write us an angel investment check back in 2005. Your kindness, selflessness, and love has been unmatched over the years. You took a bet on a bunch of young kids when you didn't have to. We're here because you got us started.

Thomas Gieselmann—for being the first institutional VC investor and backing most of our startups over 20 years. You brought us to Silicon Valley. You've seen us grow more than anyone else. There is a special joy in relationships that compound over decades, just like solid IRR. :D

Robert Simon—for being a long-time angel and supporter across all our startups. We fondly remember you dropping by the office regularly to see if the metrics were pointing up-and-to-the-right.

Omar Hamoui—for leading Sequoia's investment and backing us when things didn't go well. You were a founder first and an investor second. The empathy and founder-first mindset helped us take risks such as making acquisitions. Most VCs would've run for the hills or quietly quit. You stayed, encouraged us to fight, and saw it through.

Paul Graham—for inspiring us with your essays, your work, your advice. The longer we do startups, the more we find your advice to be true and spot on.

Josh Hannah, Pete Sinclair, Michael Mullany, Andrew Chen, Katia, and Insiya—for believing in us and sticking with us through thick and thin. Thank you for enabling us to take bigger swings and shoot for the stars.

Kevin Chou, Roger Dickey, Steven Fan, Naval Ravikant, Clinton Foy—for investing in us and alongside us for more than a decade. You're true OGs.

Siqi Chen—for being the single-greatest angel investor any founder could ask for, bar none (sorry Naval, Ron Conway, Elad Gil, Paul Graham). We don't say that lightly. You stood by us publicly when we pivoted, while others complained, criticized, or asked for their money back. When others kicked us in the teeth, you defended us. If not for your support, we would've quit years ago. You are a big reason we didn't stop at 20 or 30 pivots. Ride or die, bro; we will take bullets for you, now and always. Every founder needs someone like Siqi in their corner.

For the unsung heroes:

Mom and Dad—for doing your best to raise us. Growing up wasn't easy, and it was tough for both of you with each other. You did the best you could with what you had. We love you, forgive you, and hope you can forgive us. Each generation stands on the shoulders of those who came before, and we wouldn't be here without you. Thank you from the bottom of our hearts.

Murti: Seda, Thor, and Benji—Ho'oponopono. I'm sorry, please forgive me, thank you, I love you.

Ali: Sarah, Hasan, Emaan—for putting up with crazy ups-and-downs, mostly bad days, and long periods when I wasn't there. For dealing with uncertainty. I wrote this book so you know what I really went through. I hope this brings us closer together as a family; that this inspires Hasan and Emaan to one day go off on big adventures of their own. Family is forever.

ABOUT THE AUTHORS

Murti Hussain and **Ali Moiz** have nearly 40 years of combined experience in building online companies. Together, they co-founded companies including Peanut Labs (acquired by Dynata ~$30m), Streamlabs (acquired by Logitech ~$170m), and Stonks (current). They have raised over $50 million in venture capital from Sequoia, a16z, and others. Angel investors and mentors to founders, they hold PhDs in failure and not giving up.

Murti is a competitive squash player, surfer, aviation enthusiast, and licensed jet pilot. He lives with his fiancé, Seda, and their two dogs.

Ali enjoys writing children's books. He lives with his wife, Sarah, and his two children.

NOTES

1   OfficeChai Team, "Building a Company Is Like Eating Glass and Staring into the Abyss: Elon Musk," OfficeChai, January 12, 2024, https://officechai.com/learn/building-a-company-is-like-eating-glass-and-staring-into-the-abyss-elon-musk/.

2   Tom Huddleston Jr., "Success Requires 'Ample Doses of Pain,' Billionaire Nvidia CEO Tells Stanford Students: 'I Hope Suffering Happens to You,'" CNBC, March 15, 2024, https://www.cnbc.com/2024/03/15/nvidia-ceo-huang-at-stanford-pain-and-suffering-breeds-success.html.

3   Dale Carnegie, *How to Win Friends and Influence People*, quoted on Goodreads, https://www.goodreads.com/book/show/4865.How_to_Win_Friends_Influence_People (accessed November 11, 2025).

4   Elisabeth Kübler-Ross, *Death: The Final Stage of Growth* (Prentice-Hall, 1975).

5   Parts of this chapter are adapted from Ali's article "Stonks: 11 Pivots Later," *Medium*, June 11, 2025, https://ali-moiz.medium.com/stonks-11-pivots-later-4364dc3aa89c.

www.ingramcontent.com/pod-product-compliance
Lightning Source LLC
Chambersburg PA
CBHW032017050726
47590CB00006B/2210